Clams on the Beach and Deer in the Woods

A Collection of Oral Histories from Southern Southeast Alaska

Edited and Compiled by
Louise Brinck Harrington
Mary C. Smith

These interviews have been edited with an eye to preserve the essence of individual personalities and to offer a variety of unique memories. None of this should be taken as fact, however, as memory is a personal thing, unique to each individual. This is the beauty of oral history.

Acknowledgments

A special thank you to the folks who sat down with us and shared their stories . . . their lives, really. Our lives are richer because of your stories.

Thanks also to all volunteers who interviewed, transcribed, edited, and took pictures. Without you, this book would not be possible.

Thanks to June Allen who edited numerous interviews and kept things moving forward, writing notes such as, "Gimme more. I love doing this!" You kept us going through some frustrating times.

And thanks to John Harrington who spent hours printing and reprinting the manuscript, getting it into "book format" for the publisher. For putting up with our constant changes, corrections and additions, we appreciate you!

Table of Contents

Introduction

What a joy this book has been! Oh, we won't deny it's been work, but it's also been fun.

In 1995 we published a small book of oral histories titled *I Never Did Mind the Rain*. At that time we conducted more interviews than we could use, given a limited budget and space constraints; so we knew another book would have to be written; and thought it would be relatively easy since much of the work had already been done.

Clearly, this project took more time and energy and work than we ever dreamed. We even struggled to come up with a title. Referring to the first book, someone suggested, *"I'm Getting So Old, I DO mind the Rain."* And someone else suggested, *"Rain? What Rain?"* But like *I Never Did Mind the Rain*, *Clams on the Beach and Deer in the Woods* was another one of those phrases used by almost everyone. It may not have been those exact words but ones to that effect.

This is a you-shoulda-been-here-when book.

You shoulda been here when a handshake sealed a deal, when herring filled the harbor, when boys brought .22s to school (for shooting ducks), when girls gathered goose tongue, and when enemy submarines lurked in Tongass Narrows.

You shoulda been here when salmon was king, when fish pirates raised hell, when trap watchmen carried sawed-off shotguns, when rumrunners plied their wares and when prostitutes made Creek Street famous.

You shoulda been here when there were "Clams on the Beach and Deer in the Woods."

Stanley Bishop

We became disciples of Alaska.

Born in 1912, Stanley Bishop grew up in California where he became friendly with the Herbert Hoover family. When Hoover became president he secured a job for Stanley with the Bureau of Fisheries at the McDonald Lake Fish Hatchery. Stanley was 19 at the time. He later sent for his family and they homesteaded on the Unuk River, 60 miles north of Ketchikan on the Alaska mainland. He also farmed on the Eulachon River and prospected at Sulfurettes Creek, both tributaries of the Unuk.

For a long time I kept track of years and time and stuff, but through the years life became so complicated that I lost track 'cause I didn't think it was important to spend time worrying about which year it was.

But it was about the winter of '31. I got a few things together and sent for my mother and my younger brother and sister to come up and spend a winter with me in Alaska—before I left, before we all went back to California.

We stayed in this cabin at Yes Bay and then the next spring I went up and visited the Unuk River. I bought an outboard, but it failed me on the very first trip. I had a 17-foot dory and I rowed from Yes Bay to the Unuk. It took me four days.

That winter Harvey Matney had moved into the Unuk. He had decided to start a farm up there and had moved in all his floats and his donkey engine. He had quite an outfit. And he persuaded me to come back up and stay with him that next winter.

Stanley Bishop

I went back and told my mother, who was all for it. We got the boat loaded with groceries. Meanwhile I'd bought a little double-ender powerboat, which was our sole means of transportation. I could load the whole family's belongings in my dory and tow it behind. It was a regular old-fashioned codfish dory.

So we spent the next winter on the Unuk, and I spent most of my time cutting wood with a crosscut saw. We survived from day to day, one day at a time. Every day I cut at least two or three blocks and by late in the winter, with the freezing weather, there was about a two-inch thick rind around every log. It was just like bone; you couldn't saw it, you had to chop it off. Then you burned about three times the amount; in fact, you had to burn one wood box full to dry out enough to burn one stove full. We had wood in the oven all the time, drying it out.

That winter it got down to around eight below zero. You'd go to sleep at night and in the morning you'd wake up with your bed-clothes frozen to the wall. This little float house that Matney gave us to stay in wasn't built for that kind of weather. It had no insulation and the wind came right through the walls, through all the cracks. And wherever it found a crack your body heat would create conden-sation there and quite often your bedclothes would freeze solid to the wall. You'd have to get up and carefully pull them loose, so as not to tear the fabric.

But despite everything, Mother loved it and informed my fa-ther she wasn't going back down there to California, so he agreed to come up here. He wasn't too happy about it to start with but after a year or so he didn't want to go back to California either.

So, generally speaking, we became disciples of Alaska.

After that first winter on the river, we took up the island, our island homestead. And I had quite a time doing that because I had to prove to the Forest Service that the land was more important for agriculture than for timber. They had to come out and survey it, and any land you took out of the Forest Service had to be released by presidential signing. I forget who it was that signed mine, but they can't just say, "We'll designate this agricultural." The land has to be released and go through a lot of paper work.

And it was the same with my homestead on the Eulachon. I applied for that and it took many years. The Forest Service walked it over. They agreed it was agricultural ground all right, but then they had to go to the Territory, too, for some reason or other. And between the Territory and the Forest Service they finally gave me permission to locate it. It was an 87-acre homestead.

To abbreviate the story, when I got married, I turned the island place over to my dad—signed it over to him. Then I developed the place on the Eulachon. I brought farm equipment in, and I had 12 head of cattle and six or eight goats. During the war, I sold $27,000 worth of green stuff to a grocer in town who took my stuff on consignment.

One time I brought in a whole boatload of young turnips. They made beautiful greens, but they sat around in town here for a whole week, and nobody'd buy 'em. He didn't push 'em at all. He didn't realize these young turnips made marvelous greens. But I sold lots of rutabagas and lots of radishes and carrots and turnips and cabbages and cauliflower.

All of our ground on the homestead was flooded at least twice a year and . . . it's kind of odd. My brother and I have talked about it and we think there's something in salt water that's good for the ground. We can't raise the rutabagas down here [in Ketchikan] that we used to raise up there. No matter what you do you can't raise the same quality of rutabagas. We sold them for eight cents a pound or eight dollars a sack. I see now they're 69 cents a pound!

The Unuk River drainage is a miner's paradise. There's silver and minerals up at the headwaters of that river you wouldn't believe. And the Canadians and the big mining interests were interested in getting an outlet to the salt water. To be able to get out to salt water, that was the big thing, like Hyder and Stewart. So I worked three years on it for the Canadian Department of Public Works— building trails and working for Tom McQuillan.

McQuillan was a Canadian from Vancouver. He was interested in the same things I was. He prospected in the summer and trapped in the winter. Along toward his later years, he was much in demand. He was so, so proficient in minerals and geology.

Anyway, all of us were intent on getting a road up the Unuk—this was about 1938. We eyeballed a route up the left-hand side of the middle fork of the Unuk that would have taken us over the summit with only an 1800-foot elevation. That's the only glacier-free route and it's not a prohibitive grade. Seems to me, McQuillan told me 2 1/4 percent grade. In other words, you could have built a road up there and you could have driven a car right up.

It just made me sick when [President] Carter made it into a monument—it was such a waste of the effort we'd gone to. But that's what happened and that cut us off completely from our expectations of making the Unuk River an outlet to the sea, which these big mining companies wanted and worked for.

I had my own placer mine on Sulfurettes Creek, clear up at the head, close to 70 miles from the mouth of the Unuk. I brought placer out of that mine for three years and just scratched the surface. It was all big heavy gold, jewelry gold. The price of gold at the time was $27. I sold my gold to Gus Pruell. He gave me a little bit of an edge because it was jewelry gold and he didn't have to do anything, except burnish it up a little bit.

The strange thing about this gold was that most of it was black because it had been deposited in pyrite millions of years ago, and it had gotten black from the iron. And my first pan that I found coarse gold in, I didn't know what I had. I could see these chunks of black stuff that hung back in the pan, and I picked up a piece and scratched it on the bottom of the rusty pan. And it was *gold*. But it was as black as coal. So I put it in bottles and put in some baking soda, and after a week or 10 days, the baking soda ate most of the black off the gold.

Trapping to me wasn't work; it was a joyful thing. The smell of the autumn leaves, backpacking my stuff up the river, stopping at my cabins and sawing wood and splitting it and packing it in and smoking fish. And my old dog was with me all the time, and it was a happy time.

The dog's name was Teddy. He was my constant companion on the river. I'd had a number of dogs and most of them relied on me all the time for everything, so I told my dad, "This dog is going to

5

learn to stand on his own damn feet. I'm not going to chase around and help him across this place and that place." So I gradually started just leaving him in places that he thought was too bad to get across until he did his own job, and it gradually got to where he wouldn't wait for me at all.

That nearly turned to tragedy for him because I went across a big logjam on the main Unuk—it was just logs all crisscrossed and jammed up and fast water flowing through between these logs. And I went across on top of these logs and I looked back and he started, but he disappeared. And I waited and called, but I couldn't see him anywhere, so I was really down in the dumps. I thought, "Well, poor old bugger, he's gone." Because anything that fell in the river in those logs you'd figure they'd never get out of it. I got almost to the other side and here come old Teddy out of the water and ran up to the trail to meet me. He'd gotten through all this mess of logs and stuff ahead of me and he got to the trail and came back to meet me. And I was sure happy to see the old bugger!

I trapped mostly marten. There was a fur buyer at Billingsley's. He would buy fur, even if it might not be legal. But he had a way with him, he was so fast and so quick, and he made quick decisions. You took fur into him, he would whip through 'em, clickety-click, and give you so much for it. 'Course he graded them all right, but he'd figure up in his head and make a snap decision and give you the cash. And then he didn't want nothing to do with you and you didn't want nothing to do with him. The deal was over right there.

When I first started we got around $25 apiece for marten, and some of the last I sold I got $80 apiece for it—'course I was taking better care of my fur and prices had come up fantastically in the 20 to 30 years I'd been trapping. But at the very last I could hardly believe the prices were real.

I trapped from the mouth of the Unuk River to the Alaska boundary and I made that trip about every two weeks. Along my trap line, I had five cabins, and it took me five days to make the round trip up to my upper cabin at the boundary. And I had all these cabins stocked with food and sleeping bags and cooking utensils and tools. I couldn't carry tools or anything 'cause I had to carry bait.

I stocked the cabins in the fall while there was no snow on the ground. If there was fish in the vicinity, I'd catch fish and smoke 'em and put 'em in a cache up in a tree for trap bait. So when the season opened all I had to do was go up the line and set my traps 'cause I always left my traps hangin' on a tree.

Sometimes I would get a wolverine in one of my sets. He would think he was smart and he'd make a mistake and hit the trap the wrong way. He'd slap at a trap and try to spring it. I tell you, wolverine was my nemesis in that country. When I was baiting traps, they'd follow along right behind me, robbing all my baits. And if there was a marten that was alive in a trap they'd kill him and eat him right there on the spot.

I'd skin most of my fur at the boundary cabin—I had a pretty big cabin up there—and sometimes I'd rest a day if the weather was good and wasn't threatening snow. But if there was a storm coming, I'd keep movin' because the closer I could get to the mouth of the river the better it would be. There were lots of times I had to break trail half a day from my cabin, then go back to that cabin and stay all night. And the next day I'd have a chance to have a broken snowshoe trail half way and then I'd finish up and go to the next cabin the next day.

One winter my dad was trapping with me and we came down to six-mile and encountered a real hard snow. My six-mile cabin was small but very comfortable and we stayed there for two days and the snow didn't stop. So I started breaking trail down river, towards home. And Dad was pretty old then, he was getting close to his 80s, and he couldn't take much. This was just a couple days before Thanksgiving, and I broke trail for about three miles the second day, and it was still snowing. So I told Dad, "We'd better start now before my broke trail gets filled up again."

So we got up early in the morning and started out and we did pretty well for about three miles and then we got into snow. I had to break trail and it was pretty hard on Dad. He was all-in as we came down the Unuk River trail just across the slough from where our cabin was on the island there. And I let loose with my wolf howl— I'd usually howl like a wolf to let the family know we were comin'. And they were all out to see us.

But the tide was coming in and the ice on the slough had let loose and it was going upriver. The ice was flowing upriver. So I made a dash across the ice and the ice broke with me when I got close to shore, but I was going fast enough I made it to shore all right. So then I took a ladder and put it on the ice and I wore my skis. I stayed on the skis and I pushed this ladder alongside of me over to Dad 'cause he was just about petered out. I knew he couldn't go fast enough on the ice to keep from breaking through. I got out just about in the middle and the ice gave way beneath me—and I went under.

When I came back up, I got out onto the ice again. I got the ladder over close to the bank and I had Dad get all ready and when a chunk of the ice got close to the bank over there, I told him, "Get out as far as you can and get on that ladder." And then I alternately pulled and pushed on him and he got from one end of the ladder to the other. He'd go up to the front end and I'd move the tail around and then he'd go to the end. So we gradually got over to the bank and I got him out.

And I got out myself, but I didn't have any remembrance of being cold because when you're doing things like that you don't feel cold. Anyway, we got out and staggered up to the cabin and Mother was bustling around getting something hot for us to drink. And I remember Dad saying, "What's the matter with that root beer you were going to make?" And here he was shivering and freezing.

So my sister Betty went down and pulled the floor covering up and we dug some root beer out of the basement of the cabin. Then we sat around with blankets wrapped around us and drank root beer. And they'd made ice cream, so we had that, too.

And then we had goose. My brother Bob had shot a goose about a week or 10 days before, and they'd cleaned it and hung it up. And Mother was worried sick it wouldn't last till we got back, but it was as tender and tasty as could be. And that was Thanksgiving dinner.

My mother was a remarkable woman. She was so happy when her family was happy. 'Course I tried to build stuff as convenient as I could for her. So she was real proud of her cabin. We built it over a period of two years and it was a big cabin. The logs were peeled, no bark anywhere. We had an upstairs for Betty and Bob, and downstairs Dad and Mother's bedroom was in one corner and my bedroom in the other, and a big living room and kitchen. And it was comfortable and we always had plenty of wood ahead. Dad was good at cuttin' wood. And times when we were all together meant the most to my mother.

One time I was trapping upriver and Lloyd and Betty were on the opposite side of the river. [By this time, Stanley's sister Betty had married Lloyd Stensland.] The ice was runnin' and I didn't dare get out on the river, but on the way back I was going to call across and see if they were all right.

About half way up I run into a deer track, the first deer track I'd seen in the country. He was following a trail, going upriver, going in the wrong direction. He was getting into more and more rugged country.

I always carried an ax when I was trapping—Hudson Bay-type, about a two-pound ax with a short handle on it. And I was snowshoeing along there with this ax in my hand and I looked down and here was this damned deer down there, struggling along, still going upriver, the crazy fool. So I wasted no time at all. I threw that ax down at him and darned if I didn't hit him right in the back of the head, just perfect, just like that. And he just folded up like an accordion. All that work going upriver, and I spoiled his trip.

Poor dumb deer, I felt sorry for him after I killed him. But then I had to dress him out. I took half of the meat across the valley to Lloyd and Betty, and they had been on beans and rice for so long they said that was the most welcome meat they'd ever eaten.

There's moose around that country, too. But you're very particular about killing a moose because you can't take care of it. If we killed a moose, it was more of an organized deal than anything; we'd have things all set up so that if we did happen to run onto one and kill one, everybody'd get together and utilize him before we went back to our other work.

All in all, I've had a pretty rugged life and a lot of narrow squeaks, but I never had anything really serious ever happen to me. Seemed like it was somebody watching over me . . . because I've done things that other people only dreamed of.

And I've been very grateful for having a good family—people who would stick by you when you were drowning and you likewise would stick by them. I was lucky I had a wonderful mother. I look back and marvel at the things she did with a grin on her face.

Because in our family we were one for all and all for one. In this country you had to be.

Inga Hanson Brinck

I never minded the prostitutes and bootleggers—
they were good neighbors.

The daughter of a pioneer trader and merchant, Inga Hanson Brinck lived all her life in downtown Ketchikan. Born in 1909, the youngest of four children, she spent her early years at the Bon Marche on Mission Street and later lived at the Revilla Apartments on Main Street, after marrying the owner George Brinck. Today Inga says as far as she knows she is the oldest living Caucasian who was born in Ketchikan.

I really don't know when my father first came to Ketchikan, but he had a trading boat, the *Nettie Belle*, and he traded at all the little hamlets around here. So he must have been here quite a few years before the turn of the century [before 1900]. I wish I had talked to him more, but I lost both my parents when I was pretty young, too young to have any sense.

So I don't know how they met, how they got engaged, but they married in Juneau on January 1st, 1900. And they came right down to Ketchikan after the wedding ceremony, evidently, because all of the children were born here. My older sister Louise was born November 3rd, 1900, so they evidently didn't loiter in Juneau. And their wedding certificate is a great big large one with lots of roses.

They had a store on Front Street called the U.S. Store. It was a general store located where the Fo'c's'le Bar is now. They must have sold everything—groceries, too. I have a picture of the store with my mother and father in front, with just a little walkway in front of them, not a street. A lady came up to me once and talked to me and said, "I helped your mother when Paul was born." So

11

Inga Hanson Brinck

evidently he was born at home, and I think we all were. Doctor Story delivered all the kids.

My dad was a trader, he had the trading boat and he traded with the Indians, and that's how he got native curios and stuff. Then he'd take trips back to Chicago, and sell them. My mother ran the store when he was gone.

He built the first half of the Bon Marche in 1913, or at least that's when we moved into it. He bought the land—it was tide land—from St. John's Episcopal Church, and I think he paid $6,000 for it. It was a big piece of land on Mission Street and he only built on half of it at first; then in 1919, he built the second half, and there was a big staircase right in the middle, between the two buildings, and he joined them into one. And we had a great big porch on the back. We used to go out there and watch the ball games played on the tidelands, where the Federal Building is now—when the tide was out, of course.

We had a rowboat that we always pulled in there, back of the Bon Marche. And when the tide was high, we'd climb in it and go across the bay and have lunch. It was fun! All of us, the whole family, my mother too. She always went with us. And we'd take people from the store, we'd load the boat right down to bedrock. I remember some fishermen talking to me afterwards, and they said they kept their anchors up 'cause they were afraid we'd spill in the bay.

But we always went, to Pennock or Gravina. The sawmill was there at that time, so we'd go under the pilings and come out. And we used to watch for steamers, so we could take their wake. We liked to go swishing up and down. We thought that was a great deal of fun. Kids were easily pleased in those days.

We played a lot of cards, too. Some of the help from the store would come in and play cards at night. My father loved pinochle. Even though my mother was very religious and against card playing at first, we talked her into it. We had a lot of pinochle games and we had a lot of people around the building all the time, so we always had somebody to play with. And my mother gradually got used to it.

My dad liked to go to movies. When I was a little bit of a kid, we went to all the movies in town, my dad and I. He'd say, "We're going for a walk." I'd say, "Okay, let's go for a walk," and we'd end up at a movie. When I was in third and fourth grade, I saw a lot of movies. Freda Barron—she was, oh, not a vampire, but a sophisticated gal, kind of highfalutin'. There was the Dream Theater, the old Revilla, and the Liberty.

My mother was from Sweden and my dad was from Norway. I never did talk to them about how they happened to meet when they were both so different. He loved to *play*, and she loved to *pray*. They were not suited at all for each other. They never quarreled but they never talked to each other either and never had a room together. I could never figure it out. And I asked my mother once why she ever married him, and she said she had a bad heart, had always had a bad heart, and she needed someone to take care of her. He was 14 years older. So no fights, no disagreements, no unpleasantness, but no loving either. And of course we had the big building, the Bon Marche, so my dad lived in one end and my mom lived in the other.

I worked in the clothing department—dry goods we called it in those days. Half of the store was groceries and half was dry goods. We sold clothing to both men and women, but it was fun trying clothes on the women. We had a little dressing room, so they could try things on and see whether or not they were becoming and properly fit. And we were very honest; we didn't try to sell just for the buck.

We had a lot of full-time customers and we delivered groceries. My brothers, Paul and Ben, made deliveries and we had a deliveryman, Ed Robinson. He was an old gentleman—well, he wasn't old, I thought he was at the time—he had kind of a slow walk, a slow gait. He was with us for years and years and years, and in the early days he delivered with a wheelbarrow. And when we finally got a truck, I thought, "Oh, boy, what's Ed going to do now?"

But he could never learn to drive. They tried to teach him, but he couldn't learn. So we kept him on, but my brothers drove the truck, a Ford. Our customers would call on the telephone and give us their orders, and Paul and Ben would load up the orders in the little truck and away they'd go.

'Course we lived above the store and whenever I ran out of something, I'd run downstairs and get it and run back up. I baked a lot when I was a kid—cookies and such. And if I ran out of butter or

14

sugar, I'd run down and get it. It's a wonder I wasn't more frightened of going into a big dark store like that by myself, but I never was. We were never frightened of anything in those days up here.

'Course we lived in rather a wild neighborhood. There were some high-falutin' girls, girls who were a little *free*. Some high-falutin' girls of ill repute. And there was a building called the Rex Hotel. It was built on Main, and we were on Mission, but our buildings met there in the back. The Rex and the Bon Marche met in the back—our back ends hit. And the girls lived at the Rex.

Well, our garage had a flat roof. And we could just walk along about 8 1/2 feet of flat roof and be right next to the Rex and they had their windows right there. And so if we wanted, we could just crawl right in.

And I had a friend, Evelyn Berg; I grew up with her. We played together all the time and we'd be peeking around. And we had a back porch, so we could watch these men going in and out of the windows. Respectable people would walk down our hall—which was reliable and sensible and of no ill repute—and then they would go out our back door and get out on the porch and get into these other people's windows. And Evelyn and I would watch these men and if we knew who they were, we'd start yelling at them. We'd just see their legs kicking. We thought that was great fun. I guess kids are all the same, aren't they?

A French lady had the place next door, the Friendly Inn. She didn't have any of the girls, but she served cocktails. And she was a very charming French lady. We had a fellow working in the store, Andy Langseth. He came here from Juneau and worked all of his life here, and he died here. But he was the boyfriend of the French lady. So that's how I happened to go over there and have a few drinks— and this was Prohibition times.

We could get liquor during Prohibition because we were so close to Prince Rupert, and we all had boats. We could sneak over there and load them up and sneak back, or sometimes the fishing boats would pick up the booze and bring it over.

And, of course, we were all on tide flats at that time—this

15

was before the basement was built—so the boats could come right up to us. If you had a trap door, all you had to do was pull it up. We had a trap door at the Bon.

And during Prohibition people made homebrew. I remember going with my brothers to deliver supplies to bootleggers at Bugge Beach. Ben and Paul didn't do anything really illegal as such. They just supplied the sugar, yeast, malt and whatever else the bootleggers needed.

J.R. Heckman's was regarded as a very nice store, but if I'd ever gone there, my dad would have spanked me. They were our competitors. And we never, ever, went into any of our competitors' stores. I don't know if that would still be the rule, but we never did. Competitors weren't friendly at that time. They weren't friendly at all. Maybe my family was different, but we never associated with our competitors.

And if I'd gone into Sears, my dad would have shot me. He'd say, "Sears, they're no good, absolutely no good. They take all the business out of town, and they hurt all the small people, and they're absolutely no good!"

'Course the Sears Roebuck catalog was the Alaska Bible and everybody traded with it. They first had a little office down on Mission Street, where you could go in and order. But all my dad had to do was see that catalog and he'd throw it in the garbage!

So the only time I shopped around town was when my mother wanted meat. And I remember Mr. Patching working in the butcher shop. I don't remember if he owned it or not. And I used to go to Frye Bruhn. There were two butcher shops.

I always did the shopping for my mother, and I always paid cash. She always taught me not to buy anything unless I could pay for it. She belonged to the old school and she never used credit. I would go in the Bon Marche and plunk the cash register and mark it "house" and take whatever I needed for shopping. And I always took plenty!

I always had a pocketful of money, and we had a very nice ice cream parlor, La Follette's. So my friends and I would go there and have chocolate sundaes, and I'd pay the bill.

All through elementary I went to Main School. Then in '24 when I was a freshman, they decided to tear down the school and rebuild it. So while that was going on we went to classes downtown. We went to the Elks Club for Latin and St. John's Church for English and we went all over town. It was wonderful for me because I lived downtown. Between classes, I could run in the store and get a candy bar. Or stop at the library which was down by the M & M Bank [Miners and Merchants] in one of those little buildings, utility buildings; they're gone now.

It wasn't a very large library 'cause I read all the books. Mrs. Swineford was the librarian. She was the governor's wife—he had died—Governor Swineford. She encouraged kids to read. She'd pat us on the head, and recommend a book. I read a lot of boys' books— 'cause they had a lot of excitement in them.

I first remember George when he came to work on our stove at the Bon Marche. He was an electrician, working for Smith Electric and he'd worked for KPU, when it was Citizens Light and Power Company. And I remember him coming to our house for parties . . . with my sister Louise and her friends. He was older and in a different group so for a long time I didn't pay much attention to him.

As it turned out I knew him for 21 years before I married him. So you never know. He always liked me though. He'd come in the store and tell me how cute I was. And he'd tell everyone around, "This is the cutest little kid in Ketchikan." So he had a soft spot for me over the years.

We got married in '46, just after the war. He took over the Revilla [Apartments] I think around '34. So it's funny how things turn out . . . when people would move out of the Bon into the Revilla, I thought they were just plain traitors and the Revilla was a skunk cabbage. Because of the competition, you know. I'd get mad that people would move out of our place and move to the Revilla. Now I think the Revilla is a nice place and I enjoy living here. It's a sturdy building and will never fall down. It will be an heirloom.

Ketchikan has always been a nice place to live. It's a good little town, I think. I grew up here and had a good childhood. And the kids were always so nice. We used to play in the streets—baseball and hopscotch—because there was no traffic or anything. I never minded the prostitutes and bootleggers…they were good neighbors. So I think this is a fine place to live. I ought to join the Chamber of Commerce. Do you think they'd hire me?

Patricia Charles

Every person has a story to tell—a story worth hearing.

Patricia Charles, with her husband Paul S. (Bud) Charles, was co-publisher of the Ketchikan Daily News until 1976, when the Williams family bought the newspaper and the Charleses retired. Bud Charles and his father, Sidney D. Charles, established the Alaska Fishing News in 1934 in the basement of the Bon Marche in Ketchikan. Pat worked full-time, learning every facet of newspaper work from reporting, editing, and proof reading to backshop skills such as setting type on the bulky hot-lead Linotype machines.

I came to Ketchikan in June of 1941 on the steamship *North Sea*. I'd wanted to come to Alaska for a long time, thought it would be kind of an adventure. And truth to tell, a friend I had expected, or thought, I might marry went into the Army and . . . disappeared from my life. So I had a job with the *Alaska Sportsman* [magazine] and came to stay with my cousins, Merle and Alice Anderson. He worked for New England Fish Company.

My first impression of Ketchikan was probably the same thing that people think today, that this is a quaint little village-type town. I came from a small town too. It isn't like I was a city person at all. But it was different. I was intrigued by everything. I liked it a lot and loved the long, long days.

I grew up in the Northwest. Until I was in fourth grade we lived out in logging camps, in central Washington, upper Wenatchee Valley, and early on, in Northern Idaho. I was born in Idaho. When in Idaho my dad logged Indian land that would be just small shows, and we lived on a kind of homestead and he'd get his crew together and go maybe live in a tent if necessary. But they were small camps. Then he came over to Washington State to run a Great Northern Lumber Company camp, and that was a big camp.

Patricia Charles

But we didn't stay there too long. There was a major forest fire that more or less put that camp out of business, and then the timber market dropped. It was beginning to be the Depression and operations sort of collapsed. From then on he just took small timber, where he could buy some, and logged for small lumber companies in Cashmere.

We moved around quite a bit, but I always went to the same school, Leavenworth Public School, until I graduated from high school. Then I worked for the telephone office and did public stenography in Wenatchee. I worked other places and for the Wenatchee School District. I was secretary for the superintendent and clerk of the district. That's what I was doing when I decided to come to Alaska. It was summertime, so I could leave . . . for a summer job.

When I arrived in ketchikan, my cousins drove me from the steamship dock around town a little bit and up to their house on Water Street. And when we got to their house, I said, "Well, where's the business district?" And I'd been right through it! Their house was just across the street from Ferry's Food store on Water Street. Later my cousins bought another house that had an apartment on the lower floor, and by that time my mother Ellen Finney had moved up here so my mom and I took that apartment.

I was working for the *Alaska Sportsman*, in the office that is now the Seamen's Center, when I met Bud. *The Fishing News* published in the downstairs of the Bon Marche, and I would see him coming and going, and asked one of the women I worked with, "Who *is* that *man?*" She explained to me who he was and that he had been widowed the year before. Because we were printing the *Sportsman* in his shop, I had many reasons to be running copy back and forth across the street.

Our first date was to be December 7, 1941. Bud was going to take me out in a cruiser for the day. Then Pearl Harbor occurred and they had to put out a special edition of the paper, so that first date never came to pass, but we found other opportunities to be together.

Bud was born in Cordova. His dad, Sid Charles, came to Alaska in 1904, I believe. He had worked on newspapers in California, on the *Portland Oregonian* and in Tacoma and then went up to Fairbanks. He went over the Valdez Trail. Later his wife and two of

21

the girls came up, I guess around through Nome and up the river to Fairbanks. Later Sid worked on newspapers in Cordova, Juneau and Sitka and Petersburg and then here. He was also the marshal at McCarthy at one time.

When I met Bud, I was doing secretarial work at the *Sportsman*. I guess I was Emery Tobin's secretary. But, you know, he sold a lot of trinkets, tourist souvenir-type things and books—he sold quite a few Alaska books. So sometimes I helped to pack the books and sent out letters, mostly secretarial work. One time Emery was dictating a letter, a testimonial or something for the officer in charge of the Alaska Signal Corps, praising "your long service in the Signal Corps," and I typed it. It came out "for your long service in Singapore." That's what I heard him say. Emery giggled a little and made me retype it.

I intended to stay just for the summer, but I enjoyed my job and I liked the town. I think it was Bud that changed my mind. We were married December 18, 1943. We lived in my cousins' apartment for awhile, then rented an apartment on the second floor of the Bon Marche. We moved down there because it was just on top of our printing plant and the business. And you know that was tide flats, the building was built on the tide flats, and the silverware turned black. There were so much sulfur fumes from those tide flats that the silverware turned black.

It was an exciting time here during the war. It felt like a war zone. There was some uneasiness, and then we had the blackout and so-called bomb shelters underneath different buildings. And everything was secretive, you know, and it was hard to get news, hard to get information. Nobody could take pictures on the waterfront or of any of the vessels or anything. And they had a tower down there on the Cold Storage dock, where all the vessels coming and going were hailed. The Coast Guard manned that tower and made all the vessels coming in and going out account for themselves. We had McCarren Act passes if we had reason for being around the waterfront. We had identification cards. It was a very useful thing. I carried mine for years because you didn't ever need to show any other identification if you had one of those passes or cards.

The USO functioned for the military people to take girls to

Annette [Airfield] for dances, things like that. And you remember that old green shingle building that was down there by City Float? That was the USO building. And Mrs. McDonald, Norman McDonald's mother, was kind of the grandmother of the USO. She wrote letters for all the boys and baked them cakes. She was just a motherly person; she took care of all the young men.

There were a lot of fellows at the Coast Guard Base. And then Annette, there were Canadian fliers as well as our American pilots. And those Canadians were big on low flying. They liked to terrorize us with their doggone airplanes sometimes. But it was a military situation here, it really was.

We bought the [present *Ketchikan Daily News*] building probably in 1945. We scratched all over the place to get enough equipment, and finally did. We were able to set the paper out to publish daily, and took over the printing of the *Alaska Sportsman* in that building. Originally the place was built for the post office and then became a mortuary. Then at one time there was a union hall where the press is now—the CIO union hall was there.

We bought a press, a Duplex that came from San Francisco where it had been used to print a Chinese newspaper. That press is still underneath the floor of the *Ketchikan Daily News*. The press required a pit underneath—to be able to climb underneath it to work on it—and so before it was installed they dug a pit, built cement around that. And when it was time to demolish the press they just broke it to pieces and dropped it in the pit and cemented it over.

We lived above the plant for awhile. And then sometime in the 1950s we bought a house up on Cedar Street. In fact, Patrick was born when we lived up there. Doug was born in 1946 and Don in 1952 and Patrick in 1956. We bought the Cedar Street house from Dean Hamlin and at that particular time the pulp mill was being built and there was a real need for housing for the construction people. So Bud and Terry Myser decided they would renovate the upstairs of the Daily News into six apartments and create housing.

Over the years we had some good people in the back shop. Frank Gingg. There were Paul Saari and John Grainger. Bill Weiss, of course, he was another who was loyal and reliable and responsible, besides being so interested in youth sports. The absolutely worst thing was when Bill was working on the press, the press they have now, and got his arm caught in the cylinder. It was during a press run, and they weren't able to back it off for a period of time, and he was caught; he was trapped there. The EMT people came and gave him some sort of painkiller and Bud managed finally to get the press backed off, get him released from there and still be able to get the press running again and get that run off. I don't know how he ever did it. Bill was in the hospital for a real long time and had therapy for quite a long time. It was terrible.

One of the more exciting news stories was the big slide at Hyder, the Granduc slide. The AP sent staffers up here and they sent a photographer—his name was Doug Wilson—and they set up a photo transmitter in the ladies' room. It was an exciting time; there was something to be aware of all the time. There were boats from here— the ferry, the Coast Guard went over, the Ketchikan Volunteer Rescue Squad.

Another big story was the firebug, Bill Mitchell, and all that attended that. I remember the day when the Stedman was burning and two or three other buildings were burning and one of the firemen came up to our building and he was prowling around in the back where it was kind of dark. And I said, "Don't you want me to turn the lights on for you?" "No, I'm working in the dark here." And the firebug's method was to put a candle in some obscure place and let it burn down until it ignited something. And this is what the fireman was looking for: some evidence that a fire was going to be set.

Of course, Statehood was a major story, although our newspaper had never been particularly in favor of Statehood. We sort of argued against it, because of the small amount of land we were going to acquire. Look at it today, we're still trying to get our land situation sorted out. And it just didn't seem like the state had the resources, the development, to pay for the operations of a state. The mines had more or less collapsed, the fisheries were kind of going downhill, and the logging hadn't developed as yet. There wasn't much in the way of a tax base.

24

The biggest changes in the newspaper business since the earlier days? Well, printing methods for one thing, it's such a rapid process now. Content is different because it's not a neighborhood or hometown paper—I suppose that's bound to happen with a bigger and more transient population. And fewer news sources are as open as they used to be. We used to have access to police reports, most all courthouse filings, hospital patient lists, passenger manifests from the ships and airlines, and hotel registers. That doesn't happen anymore. It's just more difficult to print a hometown paper and I'm not sure there are enough people interested to warrant that much trudging around, getting the material and developing the sources.

My father-in-law Sid Charles always said that every person you talk to has a story to tell, a story that's worth hearing. And people are eager to tell you things. Everybody has something that they think is funny or dramatic or should be aired. If you talk long enough to almost anyone, you'll learn something that could be developed as a news story. But it takes time—it's easy enough to spend three hours talking to someone to get only a small story.

Over the years I did bookkeeping, I sold advertising and did some things with the ads, and I operated the Linotype, and then I edited, I reported.

And I read proof, even after the Williamses took over the paper and I had somewhat retired from the reporting.

But when the hot metal went and the photo offset came into being, Bud was ready to retire. He didn't want to learn that new process; he was interested in boats and packing fish and fishing crab and had lots of other interests.

Sometimes I do miss newspaper work, I think. Indeed, there were some interesting things that happened.

Torlief Dale

We'd bring .22s to school
and shoot ducks during recess.

Born in Norway December 1, 1921, Torlief Dale was a child when he arrived in Ketchikan. His was one of the many Norwegian families who settled in Alaska during the heyday of the fisheries. He says all his life people have been confused by his name, wanting to call him Dale Torlief. He became part of the Beach Gang, one of the informal groups formed by boys in those days based on neighborhood. The gangs were innocent by today's standards, but they carried on a certain rivalry in playing marbles, baseball games and feats of derring-do. Today, Torlief remembers and keeps track of his companions from his youth. He regularly hikes around Ward Lake, accompanied by some of the same fellows he chummed around with more than sixty years ago.

My mother and I left Norway and hit Ketchikan December 16, 1929. I was eight years old. My dad had been here several years, was part owner of the 103-foot halibut schooner *Helgaland*. Our port of entry was Blaine, Washington, and the other owner of the halibut boat picked us up there. My mother didn't want to leave Norway, but she finally decided she better go. My dad sent money. My mother was sick coming across the ocean. It was rough weather and she stayed in bed most of the way across. It took eight days, I think. I was busy running around the ship, the *Stavangerfjord*.

Torlief Dale

When I started school in 1930, I started in first grade. I had to learn to speak English. I was nine years old then and I was ten before I got out of first grade. We all went to Charcoal Point School until the building and dock started collapsing. The dock was our playground and a girl fell through and broke her leg. Somebody decided instead of repairing things, we'd move into White Cliff School. We had fun at Charcoal Point School. We used to bring .22s to school and we'd go down to the beach and shoot ducks during recess or lunch. We'd hang the ducks in the shed in back of the school and take 'em home with us after school.

The canneries were along there, Sunny Point and Smiley's. They had several fish traps on the beach there and we used to play on those traps. One time we were playing on them, you know, jumping on and off, running along the logs, and Bobby Bean—he was year or so older than me—jumped off this one log onto the beach. The tide was out, big flats out there, and he jumped down on a chunk of plank and there was a nail sticking up and it was sticking up through the top of his tennis shoe. So we grabbed him and the plank, all in one piece, and carried him up to the road. A kid came along with a red wagon and we hauled Bobby home in it. His dad found that the nail had come up between his toes! And Bobby was screaming bloody murder. Didn't hurt him a bit. Every time we got a chance we'd bring that up. I think they moved because of it.

We lived in a house where Madison Hardware is now, out on pilings, right at the foot of Madison Street. All fishing families along there, they were all trollers. From where Timber & Marine Supply is now all the way to the end of Bar Harbor were little homes and right alongside of each house was a boat shed. They had big doors on the waterside, and at the high tide in the fall, they'd take the poles and masts off the boats and pull the boats into the sheds, and work on 'em all winter long. And then come the big tides in the spring and they'd slide 'em out. They had moorings out in what is now Bar Harbor. The moorings had flagpoles on and their own names on them, and they'd tie up there in the summer.

And then in the spring or so, all the trollers used to load kids, canaries, cats and everything on the boats and go to Port Alexander and they'd fish out there, and they had cabins and the women stayed ashore and had gardens. My family never did that, though. My mother, Ragnhild, would get seasick just standing on the dock and watching the boat move. She was not a sailor, not at all. But she and my dad got along fine—he was out fishing most of the time.

My dad fished halibut and trolled. His name was Siguard. He had several boats. The second to last was the *Aloha*, a 57-foot halibut boat. Then he and I converted it to a troller. I trolled with him one year, and I fished halibut with him, too, but it was not my cup of tea. I liked to fish, but not commercially. Almost all the fellows I went to school with and chummed around with became fishermen though.

When I was a kid, we would go ice skating over on Gravina, on Long Lake and Bonnie's Lake. Back then we made our own fun. And skate—you could walk on your skates from one lake to another—just a little muskeg in between. We built big bonfires over there. We'd spend all night sometimes. Skate and play hockey. We'd make our own hockey sticks right there in the woods. We made 'em from hemlock trees—when they're young they come straight out and then go up. We'd bring axes and saws with us, you know, and make hockey sticks. We'd make hockey pucks out of hard wood on a lathe at the high school. We'd stash the stuff over on Gravina so we wouldn't have to carry them back and forth. There's 14 lakes in a row there! You can see 'em from the top of Deer Mountain.

Lots of kids in town, we'd hike out to Ward Lake. The CCC put in that big cabin, it was built in 1937. It's right on the plaque there on the fireplace. Bill Burns's brother worked on that, so did Butch Thomas and Joe Diamond. Charlie Whipple and Butch Thomas homesteaded up there around Connell Lake. Long before the mill came in. We used to go up there to fish, you know. The first year they put the dam across up there, a bunch of us got together and brought out a bunch of 50-gallon drums, empty, with the head out of 'em. We had a big flatbed and drove as close as we could to the dam and filled 'em with water. Then we dip-netted the coho down below, put 'em in the drums and then dumped 'em in the lake. Had a lot of fun, got soaking wet, you know . . . dip nets.

We used to fish for steelhead at Loring, right in the rapids there at the glory hole where the current comes out and swirls around there. Well, the sea runs used to come in, you know, they'd been out to sea, and if you hit it just right on the incoming tide, oh, my! Wonderful! Cook 'em right there. You gotta be dedicated to fish steelhead in the wintertime. You gotta be dressed for it, too. There you are . . . you're cold and miserable . . . and having a *wonderful* time!

I helped tear down some of the old cannery buildings at Loring. A lot of local people bought those old buildings. A bunch of us would get together in the wintertime and go out there. There was a big warehouse, huge, all made of fir. The guys would get on top and start tearing it down. Us kids used to clean the boards up, you know, take the nails out and stack the lumber. They'd make a raft of the big timbers and the boards on top of that and tow it to town. You know, those buildings along there, where Madison's yard is now, those houses all along there were built out of that lumber from the Loring cannery buildings.

As young kids, if we had enough courage, we'd go into the Spit-and-Argue and listen to the guys talk. You know about the Spit-and-Argue? That was the marine store, Tongass Marine Store, right at the corner of the dock there. And right in that very corner was the Spit-and-Argue, with the oil stove in the middle of it. Pete Bringsli was the leader of the gang there. And just around the corner on the face of the dock was the Fish Exchange, a little room where fishermen would post their hailings and the fish buyers would bid on them. Just a small room. We'd stand there and watch—one side of the blackboard for halibut, the other for salmon. Going to high school, we kids would bring our brown bag lunches and go down and sit on the dock and eat our lunch and keep track of what was going on. Watch ice coming down the chute, cut halibut cheeks—used to get 25 cents for 'em from restaurants and various people.

I worked for Doc McKenzie, the dentist, started when I was in high school. He told me I should be a dental technician. It was Jake Valentine actually taught me the trade. I worked there for several years and then when I was in the service also, part-time. I graduated from high school in 1941 and went into the Army in 1942. We were getting our draft notices so a bunch of us went out to the Coast Guard to enlist. "What's your name?" "Torlief Dale." "Where were you born?" "Norway." "When were you naturalized?" But, I wasn't. So it was good-bye, they wouldn't take me in the Coast Guard, but the Army was glad to have me.

After the war, I went back to work at the dental lab again, worked there until 1951. That next year I worked for Pat Lloyd on the *Jimmy*. We had the trap over on Percy Island. We hung the trap, as we say, over on Dall Head, that's where we kept the trap. Then we'd tow it across over to Percy and anchor it up. We'd go out and brail it every day, you know. There were a lot of big huge dog-salmon there. All the canneries wanted those dogs real bad. We sold to Independent Cannery. Ed Bugden was on the boat with me and we'd go down in the hold and we'd cut the cheeks like halibut cheeks and have a big feast. Salmon cheeks are great, better than halibut cheeks! The skipper would come down and say, "What are you guys doin' anyway?" And we'd never tell him.

Then in the spring of '52 I went out and helped build the pulp mill. I worked for the mill for 29 years. Started in what they called the finishing room, then the machine room, and ended up as bleacher man on the top floor of the highest building there, where we bleached the pulp. We made a number of grades of pulp there. Some was used for clothing, some for tires, some for dynamite, some for cellophane, and it all had different chemical composure, you know. A lot of slide rule work.

I still like fishing. Cordova Bay is an extremely interesting area. You go around Cape Chacon, on the outside, and then you go right up through Cordova Bay, up into Hydaburg, Craig, and Klawock. But it's all inside waters. In there, you've got Hunters Bay—there was a cannery there—you've got Brownson Bay, and there were canneries several of those places. Then over on the other shore you've got McLeod Bay, Datzkoo and Kaigani, just beautiful spots, really! And for beach combing, just ohhh, everything comes in those places off the ocean.

But you need to pick your weather and get the large-scale harbor charts that have every little thing marked. 'Cause there's some beautiful anchor spots, and some of them are not! You can't anchor with a southeast in McLeod Bay, for example, it just blows you right out of there.

Just think of the guys that used to row out to Forrester Island and hand-troll from Forrester Island. Row! It's just unbelievable, I don't know how they did it. And they lived on the beach! And a boat with a little gas engine would come out and pick up their fish and bring it in to the cold storage, you know.

And just imagine the fellows who came up here and explored and mapped this country. My land! They'd anchor their boats up at Tongass Island, you know, around Tree Point, and they'd get in the long boats and *row*. If they had a fair wind, of course, they'd sail, but mostly they'd row around this island, for weeks on end! No shelter, no cover on those boats, they were open like a great big skiff. And that's how they mapped this country, Vancouver and . . . I've got books about it.

But just imagine! How things have changed!

Hilda Murphy Durbin

I always liked working with people.

Elizabeth "Hilda" Durbin was born in May of 1909 and came to Alaska when she was still a child. In 1933 she married Frank "Durb" Durbin. Her son Michael was born in 1939. Frank Durbin died in May of 1988.

My name really isn't Hilda, it's Elizabeth. But I was named when my father was out of town and he didn't like the name Elizabeth, so he called me Hilda. Then when I got married, Ruthie Simonsen put Hilda Murphy on our marriage license. I always told her we weren't really married—I could actually leave anytime 'cause we weren't really married. I reminded Ruthie of that the other day!

My parents were Agnes Bruce Murphy and Jerry Murphy—Jeremiah Murphy, I beg your pardon. And we came from Massachusetts, and from Seattle to Petersburg on the *Humboldt*. And I don't think anybody remembers the *Humboldt*. It was a steamer, but from the way my mother talked, it wasn't a very big one. Agnes and Mama were sick all the way, and I was just having fun. There were eventually seven of us, two boys and five girls. Hilda, that's me, Agnes, Ann, Mary, Tish, Jerry and Mike. Tish is really Patricia and Jerry is Jeremiah.

My dad was a halibut fisherman from Newfoundland. He fished the Great Banks, I think is what he called it. We went to Petersburg, and I don't remember too much about it, but they had a shrimp cannery there. I went down there one day and asked for a job. There was a Chinese man, he gave me a nickel. His name was Sing Lee. He gave me a nickel and I peeled the shrimps—they were cooked—and I ate them. I thought that was nice of him!

Hilda Durbin

Then we came to Ketchikan. Let's see, '09, '10, '11, '12, '13, '14, that should have been 1915. I started first grade that year in Petersburg and finished it in Ketchikan.

The school was right up this hill, Austin Street, a little red schoolhouse, up on the hill there someplace. I think it burned down later, I'm not sure. And it was a pest house for a long time. If you got scarlet fever or something, they put you in the pest house. We had to stay away from it, it was quarantined.

I went up town to Main School for the fourth grade. The reason I remember fourth grade is because Miss Chapman was my fourth grade teacher. And she pasted my mouth shut with adhesive tape. I reminded her of that one time and she said, "Oh, Hilda, I never would have done a thing like that!" I remember I was talking to a fat boy that was living with his grandmother here. What in the world was her name? She lived in Indian Town, a little Jewish lady. She was really an oldtimer. I think she used to go bail bond for all the bootleggers. Wish I could remember her name.

There was an old lady name of Mrs. Abercrombie that had a millinery store by where the tunnel is today, on the town side, Grant Street, coming down from Main School. I don't know why she ever put up with us 'cause we used to go in there and try on hats. That was a lot of fun! I don't think I ever had any money. I was just in there to try on hats. She used to have white mice in there and she would give permanents, do your hair. When I got big enough I'd go in every once in awhile and get a permanent. That was a funny store!

We always had fun. I remember jumping on the back of the coal wagon! It was horse drawn. And I thought I was just really and truly doing something tricky, jumping on the back for a little ride. Of course, you know it wasn't going very fast.

And someplace down around here they used to have a wire works. They used to have these great big rolls of wire, for fish traps. You've seen them. We used to go over there to play and jump on those things like a bunch of trampolines. You can imagine how good you could jump on those things. That was a lot of nice clean fun and we didn't get dirty on those things. Didn't get scratched. All the bad ends of the wire they must have rolled underneath on account of we never got hurt on them, but then it never occurred to me that you could get hurt!

When I got to be a teenager we'd go down to the dock and meet the boats and see all the people coming off. Sometimes you'd go aboard and they'd feed you cake and coffee. That was kinda fun. There was the *Dorothy Alexander*—used to come in here every June 9th. They'd always have a dance when they came in. They would just stay here a matter of hours, in the middle of the day, but they'd have a dance.

And I loved to dance. There were Scandinavian dances every Wednesday at the old Eagles Hall, where the Red Men are now, and regular dances at the Red Men Hall, where it was then before it got burned down, in that parking lot by the side of the Coliseum Theater. I liked both of them real well. They just didn't have enough dances for me! There was Williams that had a band, he always played at the Red Men Hall. And they usually had a squeeze box and a piano. That was good fun! And I could only go to the Scandinavian dances when my dad was out of town. I don't know why he didn't want me to go to those dances. As soon as he was out of town I was back there again!

I learned how to dance at La Follette's. It was an ice cream parlor. We'd go there during our lunch hour. I never took lunch to school. I would go to La Follette's and have a green river [lime and 7-Up], I think it was a dime. A bunch of us kids would go down there and they had a music box. And we'd play these records and dance down there.

One day my father passed by—there was a little alley—he walked past there and looked in and there was Hilda dancing her little ol' head off. And he said, "You cannot go to La Follette's anymore." So I was never allowed to go there anymore. And all I had was a green river. I don't think they served anything else. Green rivers and that kind of stuff.

They had a skating rink downtown, too. They called it the Hippodrome, and I wasn't allowed to go to that either. I think my dad just liked to let us know who was boss. We weren't allowed to go to Indian Town either. Well, there was a party down there one time for a Japanese girl and I wasn't allowed to go, but I went anyway.

36

And Creek Street. I never knew why they made Dolly's house down there such a thing. She was the silliest-looking old lady I ever saw. Little blonde curls. She had a bunch of dogs and they looked like her! Pomeranians, I think they were called. They had little squashed faces. And Dolly had a little tiny voice, her voice didn't sound at all like she should sound. She didn't look like she should sound like that. I don't have any idea how come we called them "fancy ladies." I guess they were always dressed so nice and they always smelled so good. Perfumed and powdered and dressed to kill.

How'd I meet Durb? I was working at the cannery and he was driving a cab. I used to see him as he drove past as I was coming home, and I thought he was kind of cute. And he made eyes at me, or I made eyes at him, I'm not sure which. But we did get acquainted. He owned the yellow cab, the Yellow Taxi. They weren't allowed to call it Yellow Cab; they had to call it Yellow Taxi. And it was certainly busy. The picture there of the cab, with the 1935 license plate, parked outside the Kentucky Liquor Store—we owned that, too. That's where the phone calls came in, phone number 98. There was a sign over the liquor store that said "If the kids need shoes, don't buy booze." It was a big sign and an awful lot of tourists took pictures of that sign!

Michael was born in 1939 and I didn't go to work until he was old enough to go to school. He would come home and be there about an hour before I came home. I was a waitress for about 17 years, I worked at the Del Mar and at the Stedman Café and other places. I liked working with people, yeah, I still do. I'd work at one place for two or three years and then move someplace else. That was kinda fun. Yeah, and then I went to work for the ferry system in 1964 when I was 55 years old!

I worked at the Federal Market, downstairs, and then Mrs. Rollog asked me to work in the office. And I didn't know anything about that, and she said, "Well, we'll teach you." So I did that. I had to cash out all the time and find mistakes people had made on their tapes. So that was fun, but I told the Rollogs I'd like to go back down to the cash register, down where the people were. I didn't really like being away from people.

I was working there, at the Federal, when Bill Mitchell came back to town and set fire to all those places [in 1961]. He set fire to the building that backed up to the Federal Market. So we were busy, running stuff down and getting it out to the front. Because the fire was burning right in back. That Bill was naughty. He was always the first one at the fires, though. He knew where they were. I think he did it for pure enjoyment. He'd do it on any kind of celebration day, like his birthday and the Fourth of July.

One time he came to the Federal Market and he was complaining about something. And he said for a certain amount—he said it jokingly—he said, "Would you like to get rid of this place?" But he was joking . . . I think.

Another time he came into the store and I wasn't right at the cash register. But I saw him wave or say hello or something. And on his way out he hit a button on the cash register. And then a lady came along and got a loaf of bread. And I went back to the cash register and rang it up and it came up $100.38 or something like that. And the lady said, "Oh, my goodness!" And I said, "Oh, but this is really good bread."

I was married to Durb for 52 years, I think it was, and it was kinda fun. I did what I wanted to do and he did what he wanted to do, and we made that arrangement. He never did learn to dance. His feet didn't work right. We tried it a couple of times. If he'd stayed home and let me teach him, that would have been fine. But he didn't want to do that. He wanted to practice with someone, a good dancer, on the dance floor. But that didn't work.

One time my brother Jerry and one of his sons, Bud, came back up and visited us. And they wanted to go out on the town and asked if I wanted to go. I said I'd love to go. I was always ready to go out. So we went and had a marvelous time. I took them down to that place that used to have sawdust on the floor, the Frontier, and then to the 108, and then to another place. And they both knew how to dance so I had Bud and Jerry both. We really had quite the evening.

You know, years ago, there were no strangers in town. And you said hello to everyone. Everyone you saw. Now it's terrible, you go downtown and you don't know anybody anymore. But a long time ago you knew them whether you knew them or not. Even if you'd never seen them before, you said hello and kept on going. They were in town, so you said hello to them. At least I always did.

Ken Eichner

I worshipped airplanes since I was a child.

Ken Eichner was born in South Bend, Washington on June 8, 1918, the day of the total eclipse of the sun. He is a fine example of a man who succeeded in combining his vocation and his avocation. By doing what he enjoyed he developed a profitable business, now called Temsco Helicopters. He also made an important contribution to the community with his part in the Ketchikan Volunteer Rescue Squad.

I always wanted to fly. When we moved from Washington [State] to Lebanon, Oregon, I was eight years old. And those were the days after World War I when you could buy a Jenny airplane for, I think it was $600. And the plane was all crated up and you could get it shipped on the railroad right to your hometown. Well, some of our neighbors bought one and they rigged it up and taught themselves to fly. And they would taxi down the field and jump in the air a little bit and then got so they could jump over a fence and then finally they could fly.

My heroes were the famous pilots like Tex Ranken and Dorothy Hestor who used to do outside loops and do a 100 of them in a row. And they'd come back with their noses bleeding and ears bleeding, but bragging, "Boy, I did it!"

I had been going to the University of Oregon but got hurt playing basketball and couldn't go back to school. We kids always idolized our uncles who fished and trapped and hunted in Alaska and all the wild stories they told. So when I went to Seattle and asked my uncles if a buddy and I could ride to Alaska with them, they said sure.

Ken Eichner

So we all came to Ketchikan on my uncles' fish packer the *Estrella* in April, 1938. They took us out to Johnson Cove on Etolin Island where they had their summer camp and their fish traps. We helped them get the traps ready to go and then they brought us to town and said goodbye.

I was 20 years old and my first residence was 10 Hopkins Alley, a one-room shack with running water just outside the door. At that time the downtown streets were planked and the two big ship-yards, Northern and McKay, were the most prominent structures. There were buildings all along the water side of downtown. And there were wooden docks and later on during the war, freighters would regularly ram the dock and knock out pilings here and there. One time one of the boats run clear up into Kubley's soft drink fountain. They were single-screw boats and when they tried to make a star-board landing, they often had trouble.

But I was thrilled to be in Alaska and trying to make a living. I would build rock walls and I worked for a lady out in the Bugge Beach area. She had a chicken farm and once a week I would clean her chicken coup and do physical work around her place and she would give me a dozen eggs and feed me lunch, and sometimes give me 50 cents. I remember bumming halibut off the dock. Finally I got a job driving cab, a '36 Plymouth, for White Cab and Bus Company owned by Charles E. Pollack and Bill Easton.

Then I got advanced to bus driver and I was driving an old '35 Ford which hauled about 16 people, when I met Peg. She was working at the school; she was a secretary at Main School. And she would ride my bus. So we got acquainted that way, and sometimes she would make the whole round trip out to Smiley's Cannery with me.

We got married August 3, 1939. Our first home was in Foss Apartments. There were eight apartments and we lived in one of the front ones. You could look right over the water and I remember one morning we woke up and a Liberty Ship was hung up on one of the rocks right out in front. When the tide came in, it floated off all right.

Danny was born May 1, 1941 and Suzie September 4, 1943.

I'd always been in the National Guard and the R.O.T.C. at the University of Oregon, so when I came to Alaska I joined the Territorial Guard. There were probably 40 of us, including the captain Dick Hogben, Ed Dorn, Bob Strong, John Minnich, Al Hansbury and Skip Thompson's dad. We did our own training. We had some old World War I equipment, helmets and Enfield rifles, and we had a bunch of wire that we could string out for a little telephone system. But we were going to fight the Japs if they came. And when Dutch Harbor was bombed, we got serious and started caching stuff in the hills.

At the time of the draft, I was deferred because I was in the bus business and had a family. I was 3A. But they said if I did get drafted and if I had a pilot's license, I could fly when I got in the service. I might not be a fighter pilot, but I would fly something. So I learned to fly at the old Ketchikan Air, run by Stan Oaksmith and Ben Smith and Howard Beamer. That was in '44.

I got my license in '45 and in June of that year I was called up and sent over to Annette Island. But then the war was over in Germany, and it ended up I didn't have to go. But I wanted to be a fighter pilot in the worst way, 'cause I worshipped airplanes since I was a child.

During the war I continued to drive bus. Then Al Hansbury and I decided to buy out Claude Pollack, and Dewie Barber bought out Bill Easton. So we took over the White Cab and Bus Company. And when we separated the buses from the cabs, we renamed it Northern Bus Company. That had to be in 1941. We started the service station on our bus property [2450 Tongass Avenue] in 1954. It was one of the first stations with full service in Ketchikan.

After maybe five years of running the buses and the service station, we sold the city bus service to one of our drivers. We kept the main Northern Bus and the school buses and eventually moved out here to North Tongass, Mile 4 1/2.

Then in 1958 I started Temsco. It was a 24-hour a day business and I ate and slept Temsco—and enjoyed every minute of it. And when the tough trips came along I took them instead of letting someone else. Because after the Pan American crash in 1947 Dick Borch and I had started the [Ketchikan Volunteer] Rescue Squad.

One of the first rescues I took part in was in 1943 when I was still with the Territorial Guard. Harold Gillam was a famous Arctic pilot. He was coming up from Seattle. He had a Coast Guard man aboard, a Fish and Wildlife official, and two older gentlemen from Fairbanks and Anchorage, V.I.P. persons; and he had a new secretary for the CAA, now the FAA. He was flying a twin engine Lockheed Electra like Amelia Earhart flew.

He left Seattle and for some reason or other lost an engine on the airplane and became disoriented. I think they had changed the leg of the beam for Annette Island. And he was coming to Annette to make a fuel stop. And I'm not sure whether the other engine crashed or whether he was unable to hold altitude, but he crashed into the trees at the 1800 foot level at Boca de Quadra.

And the young girl, the young secretary, her arm was severed; and she lost too much blood and died the first night. The two older men were injured. Gillam survived the crash, but had a concussion. And this was in February, the coldest winter we had ever had. The survivors spent three days up on the mountain. But the weather was so bad all the airplanes involved in the search went over or under, but never where they were. So Gillam decided he would hike to salt water.

He had a parachute and a little food with him (the airplane was well stocked with tents and sleeping bags and everything) and he hiked from Weasel Cove clear out almost to the entrance of Quadra. But apparently he overexerted himself. He wrapped up in his parachute, lay down to go to sleep and froze to death. But before he did, he hung up a yellow streamer out on a limb overhanging the water.

Anyway 30-some days passed and finally one of the Coast Guard boats was down in Quadra, getting out of a storm. And they saw these two guys on the beach with a bonfire, jumping up and down and waving. The Coast Guard didn't think anything of it. But the next morning the fire was still burning and the guys still jumping up and down and waving, so they went over and here were the two younger fellows that survived the crash.

Well, they brought those two fellows to town and got a search party to go get the others. The fellows said that the closest access was from Smeaton Bay. So 18 or 20 Coast Guard people hiked in to the survivors, but they weren't prepared for the cold weather and they got in there and they were marooned. Well, two of them hiked out and told of the predicament. So they sent the [USCG Cutter] *Cedar* down there and they called for the Territorial Guard to come help out and half a dozen of us from the Guard went along.

We got down there at Smeaton Bay and two fellows came out of the woods and told us they thought it was closer to go on the other side. At the same time, a Navy Kingfisher arrived with a pilot by the name of Gil Joint. He flew over the crash site and saw the predicament these guys were in and they had stamped out in the snow "SEND A BLIMP." Well, there wasn't a blimp within a thousand miles of here. So that was out.

So Gil Joint picked up [Coast Guard man] Bruce Johnstone and landed him on the other side into Badger Bay. Bruce took an axe with him and walked across the ice and up to the crash site within an hour, whereas these other guys had been hours hiking up the other way.

So Captain Burns who was the skipper of the *Cedar* took it out and around and into Quadra. I was on the front deck and, as we were going around, I spotted that yellow streamer. I waved and hollered at them and they stopped the boat. Jack Johnstone, Bruce's brother, and some other Fish and Game fellow went ashore and found Gillam's body and brought it back aboard the boat.

Well, we went on up to Badger Bay, which was froze solid. The *Cedar* rammed it to try to break in so we could get in closer, but that didn't work. Gil Joint with his Kingfisher dropped two bombs and they just went plunk, they didn't do anything. So then we decided the only thing was to hike in. We only had one toboggan with us and we took it up to the crash site and were gonna bring just the one guy out. But the other fellow said, "Shoot me, but don't leave me here another day." So we improvised another toboggan and we brought both of them out.

They left the girl's body in the airplane for the winter. And the next spring Ray Renshaw, a local pilot, hiked up to the wreck and helped bring the girl out. And he told me later that it really struck him because she was such a beautiful girl.

Now when the Pan American plane crashed, that was my first aerial search. My search pattern was the Mirror Lake area. And I can't remember who first spotted it—the big tail was still left there on Mount Tamgas.

But anyway Dick Borch was the ground crew. And he was probably one of the strongest individuals and so talented at being able to take care of himself in the wilderness, to survive. I remember Roger Elliott flew him with a Grumman into the closest, smallest lake they could get into. And then it was all straight uphill from there. And then they brought the bodies out, something like 20 or so.

Well, after that Dick and I got in on every search that came along. They were hollering for me because I was my own boss and could take off when I wanted to. And of course I would rather fly than do anything. My partner at the company, Dewey Barber, and I had bought a small T-craft from Ketchikan Air. That was our first airplane and we got to do a little hunting and fishing and thought we were pretty important. And so I was available for search and rescue with that little T-craft right off the bat.

Dick always had his radio on channel 16. So anything that would come up, he was listening. And the Rescue Squad at that time didn't have rapport with the troopers, so we acted on our own. Dick would glean what information he could over the radio and call the Coast Guard. Then he would call me. And I was 100 per cent available, first with the airplane, then the helicopter. And Dick was always ready and wherever he was working, they always let him go. If he had to, he would quit a job just to go on a rescue.

So I had the transportation end and Dick was the ground end, and between the two of us, we pretty well covered it. At that time we got no help out of the government. The troopers for some reason or another didn't have money to spend for search and rescue. Later on they finally did, but I had a standing rule with them. We're going on this search whether you're paying or not. If you feel that it's justified afterwards, then you can pay us, if you don't, don't. And I know that a lot, especially medivac, we never got paid for—$30,000 worth one year.

One of the first rescues I did was with the airplane. I made a night flight into upper Goat Lake. [Pilot] Margie Ross had taken two fellows goat hunting. They had gone up to the top of the mountain and killed a goat and one fellow was elected to carry the goat down to a different lake. And Margie and her other hunting partner were going to go down to the airplane and fly to upper Goat Lake to pick him up. And so she flew to upper Goat Lake and there was nobody there. And so she flew to the lower lake and now the weather is starting to go to pieces. It's starting a southeaster. And so she dashes to town and gets in just before dark and has to get somebody to go rescue him.

So I took my airplane and one fellow with me and we took sleeping bags and stuff to spend the night. And we went and looked over the area that she said they had started from. We saw a little flicker. The guy was trying to light his lighter. All we could see was the flint. So we went over to the beach and here's this guy, so cold he can't move. We got him in the plane, and the two of us sat there and hugged him until we got him so he could start talking.

But I've flown over people in the woods and they can see me but I couldn't see them because they were in the woods and didn't have anything to wave. All you have to do is to get out in the open and lay something in a straight line or a cross to attract the eye. If there's water around and someone is flying over you, throw a rock in. You always see a fish jump. Or you make smoke. So it's those simple things.

When it came to prospecting I was not very smart. But because I had the airplane, I got acquainted with old Jim Pitcher who had been on the Chilkoot Trail and had seen all of the gold rush. Well, at that time he was quite crippled, so I'd take him out and we did various things, like staking a bunch of uranium claims up in Salmon Bay. And one time I found rock that had beautiful copper in it and Jim was all set to start a mine, but we went back up and it was just in one rock, you know. That was the only rock that had the copper in it.

And I have a little mine up in El Cap that was found by An-gus Lilly, one of my prospecting partners. He worked it with Homer Pitcher in the '30s. They would get beautiful specimens of gold out of it, and everybody who looked at it said it was a contact deposit and that vein should go forever. But we couldn't find it forever. When gold wasn't worth much, we didn't pay much attention to it. And all of a sudden gold was worth $800. So we leased the prospect to these guys and they drilled, but they didn't drill in the right places. Then gold dropped in price and they backed off. And then we had a mining geologist and he was convinced that it was a contact deposit. So I finally spent the bucks and drilled in the right places, but it's not big enough to be a mine. You can find pieces of gold, just sticking out there, just beautiful, but not enough to make a mine. I have wanted to patent the land, but now with the regulations, there's no way to do it.

We had these claims up on the Bradfield, too. And though it's remote, there is gold there. So I still think there's a possibility that someday, somebody will mine it.

We have grandchildren and great grandchildren now and one of my grandchildren is flying for Temsco—Dan's son, Eric. And it's very rewarding to have him thank me for my guidance and help in getting his license. There're so many guys that come and tell me, "Oh, yeah, you gave me my first airplane ride," or, "You gave me my first helicopter ride." Well, you see I used to be the Boy Scout master and I'd take all the scouts for a ride. A whole generation of kids—and a lot of them went on to be airline pilots.

For myself, I enjoyed every minute of Temsco, the search and rescue. It was the excitement both in the outdoors and living and growing up in the business. You do everything the best you know how, and that's it. I got accomplished enough to where I could go into small lakes and do everything with my best judgment. And then the things you learn to do in this country. For instance, you fly into fog, you fly close to the water, and when it gets to where you can't see a given distance ahead, you land, you taxi. And if it lifts, you fly again. And you never make a turn under those conditions. Those are the things that keep you alive.

But the opportunities here are something you don't find everyplace. Alaska is a tough place but, for me, it was a challenge.

Bob Gore

They brailed me outa the fish trap!

The Gore name is known all over Alaska, from Bob's travels for the Pioneer Home Advisory Board and from his great- great-great-grandfather (not sure how many "greats") who sailed with Captain Cook. The name spread from Gore Point to Gore Island to Gore Mountain. Bob says, "When we were looking for property outside of Seward [for the Pioneer Home Advisory Board], they told me I was the first Gore they knew of being there at Gore Point for 200 years!"

I was born in Ketchikan on the sixth of June 1928. My father Lester Gore was an attorney here at the time. He first came to Alaska in 1913 when we got territorial status. He'd just gotten out of Law School at the University of Washington. Adolph Ziegler, Bob Ziegler's dad, talked my dad into coming up and taking this job—what they called the United States Attorney for the Juneau District. At that time my dad lived in Juneau.

He came down here in, I think, 1923, and went into private practice and met my mother. My mother Irene was a French Canadian girl in town visiting her sister Cora Rivard, who was the wife of Jules Rivard. According to [Newspaper Publisher] Lew Williams, Rivard started the first newspaper in Sitka and the first newspaper in Ketchikan.

My mother was a violinist. One of the things she did just for entertainment was she and a lady who played the organ and another lady formed a little band and they provided dance music down there at the place where the Ketchikan Garage used to be. The place that had a maple dance floor. And then they also played at the Coliseum Theater for the silent movies.

Bob Gore

After my parents got married they stayed here in Ketchikan until 1932 when my dad was appointed Federal Judge in Nome, so we moved up there and I had the time of my life. That was a great place. I had a little friend who had a dog team. His father was a trapper called "Big Joe" and this "Little Joe" was my pal, and we used to go all over the country up there with his team.

And because my dad was a judge, my brother and I got to do a lot that other kids couldn't do. My brother was two years older than me, and his name was Charles Millard. We called him Millard after my dad's brother.

Anyway, all the mail was at that time delivered by dog sled, out to the mining camps, you know. And the driver's name was Chuck O'Leary—he had the contract to deliver the mail. And every now and then he would go up to my dad's office and tell him, "If you want to get rid of the boys for a couple days, I'll take them out on the run with me."

So Chuck would pile us in the sled with the mail sacks and cover us up with reindeer skins, polar bear skins, whatever he had. And then he'd tie everything down, and us too. And he had 12 dogs, a big team. We had a good time growing up there.

My dad and his brother were "water men" because my grandpa Charlie was a marine engineer and a riverboat pilot, too. Grandpa Charlie had a pilot's license for the Columbia River and also a chief engineer's license for steam engines. So, growing up, my dad and his brother used to ride back and forth on the boats, the steamboats, from their home in Kalama, Washington up to Portland, Oregon.

Grandpa Charlie was up here before the gold rush. He came up under contract to the Hudson Bay Company to operate one of their river steamers called the *Beaver*. They were hauling supplies from Wrangell up to Telegraph Creek. The proposed Trans-Siberian telegraph line was under construction at the time. They were running up to Telegraph Creek and then further up the Stikine [River] to drop off supplies and build the weigh station. Anyway, they were up there all summer and, in the meantime, the sandbar at the mouth of the Stikine had changed to the point that when they came down the river in the fall, they ran aground. So Grandpa Charlie and some other guys stayed up there to salvage the machinery out of the ship.

And my dad told me that at that time the Stikine Indians were kinda ferocious and they wanted to come out and salvage what they could off the ship, too—just steal it, you know. So my grandpa and these other guys stayed up there to get everything ready to haul out. They were going to get the engines out, put 'em on rafts and get them to Wrangell and then haul them south. Which I guess they managed to do.

Anyway, we left Nome in the summer of '35. My sister Nancy—Nancy Murkowski—was born up there and my mother wanted to get us kids back to Ketchikan to school. The canned salmon industry was just becoming organized and they wanted my dad to do the legal work—my dad and Judge Arnold who had been law partners here. Arnold had stayed here and lived in our house up on the top of Bawden Street while we were in Nome.

But it was quite a trip back. We were crossing the Gulf of Alaska and one of the worst storms, the first winter storm, rolled in. We were getting ready to go down for breakfast and my dad went down first to get a cup of coffee. And he came back up to the cabin and said, "You may as well stay here 'cause the water has been so rough the top came off the galley range and they're not cooking anything today until they get it fixed."

But they got it fixed and we kept on goin'. And I remember when we got down to Kodiak, we saw green trees for the first time. And then in those days we had to go all the way down to Seattle and then take a boat back to Ketchikan. After crossing the Gulf, they went around on the outside right straight to Seattle. But we made it back up here in time for school.

And we were here in time to see the salmon industry develop and work our way into it. I started out on tugboats and cannery tenders, when I was 14. My dad had a deal worked out with the school 'cause he was the attorney for the cannery down there at Hidden Inlet, the Nakat Cannery that we all worked for. So we got out of school early. They'd have a plane ready for us to go to Hidden Inlet on the 17th of May every year, a couple weeks before school was out officially.

We'd break it in down there and did all the pre-season work like getting the wire ready for the trap and patching up all the seines and webbing that they used in the traps and seine boats and so forth. During the season they'd get all torn and worn so we'd replace and repair and get them ready to go in the traps and get the seines ready to go in the boats.

For three years I worked on a seine boat that belonged to my dad. After we came back from Nome, the federal Fish and Wildlife had been getting all these complaints from independent fishermen about how the canneries owned all the traps and most of the seine boats. So the feds said that the canneries had to put some of them out to private ownership. It was a better spread of the industry. That's when Dad bought two fish traps and two seine boats.

So in '49 and '50 and '51 I seined on my dad's boat, the old *Valentine*. She was run by a native skipper named Andy Moses. Andy taught me lots of things. If you're gonna go out trapping and your traps have rust on them, or if your rifle is getting rusty, he said you go out and dig up a bunch of skunk cabbage roots. And you put them in a great big pot and you boil it and you put your traps in there and your rifle in there and it takes all the rust off. But it turns the metal brown. It's just like bluing, except it's brown and it keeps the rust off, and it takes the human smell off.

He said if you get a stomachache, or your heart hurts, you take a lot of roots off the devil's club and you make tea out of them. You boil them and you make tea and you drink it. Yeah, Andy ended up adopting me—I had a white father and an Indian father, too. And I learned it all from guys like Andy Moses, guys that were good.

Bob Bushre was an ex-Coast Guard Officer and he was skipper of the old tug, the *Chilkoot*. And he taught me navigation and how to chart a course and about boat work and engine work, and about fish traps.

One time we were brailing a trap down around Cape Fox and I was standing on one of the logs on the trap frame, pulling up the web—to bring the fish up to the surface, you know, so they could be brailed out. And that's down by Dixon Entrance and there're funny waters down there, and a big wave came in and came over the trap frame and just hit me right in the butt and shoved me overboard into the inside of the trap.

But I'm a survivor.

I was in there with a lot of these fish and I just started swimming. And then they brailed me outa the trap with the brailer. The guys on deck pulled me out and stood me up. Later Bushre told me, "We saw you going in and when you came out we thought you were Jesus Christ returning, because you were walking on water!"

Another time with Bushre, we were towing a log raft out of Abe Lokke's camp on the Chickamin [River]. And coming back into the spruce mill we hit a storm coming up Clarence Straits and running up Behm Canal. And the lashing that fastened the boom into the top of the cradle worked itself loose and every time we hit a big swell the boom would come up and then down on top of the cradle, and it was starting to crack up the top of the cabin.

I told Bushre, "Well, it was probably my responsibility to make sure that thing was made fast before we took off. I guess I better go up and tie it down." And he said, "Well, I was going to suggest that." He said, "You don't have to, but you're the youngest and the toughest and probably the most agile. It will take somebody to climb around and not get blown off or washed off when you're up on top." He said, "Put on a life jacket. I'm going to tie a line around you and you climb up the ladder on the side of the cabin, and I'll just feed out that line so we'll have some way to haul you back in if anything happens."

We were takin' water over the bow and over the top of the house and everything. But I felt awful brave at first. I thought, "Hell, I can do that." At that age you feel you can do anything.

I got up there and I was holding on with my eyebrows, teeth, toe nails and finger nails. And when I got back down I realized just how scared I was. You don't get scared on things like that until it's over. When I got back down I did admit it was just a little scary up there.

One year before the fishing season, Ernie Steers was looking for somebody. He had the old *Chief*, probably one of the oldest tug-boats in Alaska and she acted like it too. Her engine was always acting up. Jack Abegglen was also aboard. I was cook, deckhand and engineer. Jack was deckhand, but we split the work all the way around.

We were towin' a raft and we were in Clover Pass. As we came by Grant Island, I was at the wheel and happened to look over my shoulder out the window in the back of the pilothouse and I saw this black thing in the water. It looked like a box 'cause there were a couple of corners sticking up on it. I put the glasses on it. It kept getting closer to the raft. Way up in the front of the raft they have these headers shaped like a kind of V. Anyway, this old black bear climbed up there and sat down on the head log. He was looking around and so forth, enjoying the ride.

Ernie had a bunk in the back of the pilothouse. He opened his eyes and said, "What are you looking at?" I said, "A little black bear just climbed up on board the raft and I'm just watching it."

"A black bear? On our raft?" I said, "Yeah." He said, "You're crazy!" I said, "Here, the glasses. Look." He came out of bed and looked back there and he said, "By God, there's a bear on the raft." So he says, "I got to get a picture of that."

I got to digress a little bit. It was right about the Fourth of July, a day or two before, and Jack and I were bugging Ernie about getting back to town in time for the Fourth. So when I took over the wheel, I had asked Ernie what kind of speed we were makin'. He said, "Well, we're makin' between four to six knots, maybe a little more. Don't worry about gettin' back in time for the Fourth, we'll make it."

So anyway, he woke up Jack and they took the skiff off the back of the boat and they had to row back to the raft to get a picture of the bear. But the bear saw them coming and jumped off and swam past us. And about that time the two guys rowed back to the boat and came on in the pilothouse. And I couldn't help it. I said, "Hey, Ernie, if we're making six to eight knots, you know we just got passed up by a 10 to 12 knot bear!"

Ernie said, "Damn kids. You're going to get off the boat and go back with Bushre as soon as the fishing season starts, aren't you?" I said, "Yeah, I am. I told you that when I came on board."

He said, "Well, you might as well get off the boat now on this trip. Besides that," he said, "you can't make very good gravy." I said, "Well, I was never a gravy maker anyway." Because all he liked to eat was fried pork chops and fried potatoes. I said, "Nobody ever taught me to make gravy." He said, "Well, you make it out of what's left in the pan after you get everything fried." I said, "That's just grease. I've been pouring it overboard." He said, "It's good for you."

I said, "Well, you better tell Jack to get his mother to show him how to make gravy then when we're in town, because I'm not coming back. You told me that." He said, "Well, maybe Bushre can put up with you. I can't."

That was the first and only time I ever got fired—'cause I couldn't make good gravy.

But that was a good way to grow up, just good clean living. You worked hard and you worked long, and you came out of it with a feeling that, hey, I can do anything—anything that needs to be done. And [even today] if I'm on my way to do something that has to be done, well, don't get in my way, 'cause even with this broken hip, right now, I can get anywhere I want and I can do anything I want. I don't go too fast, so if you see me coming, get out of my way, because I don't want to be slowed down.

Like I said, I'm a survivor.

Marie Henn

We picked goose tongue on the beach

Marie's husband, Henry Henn, always said he came to Alaska to find Marie. Though this is mainly Marie's story, it is one of enduring devotion, for she and Henry were married for 75 years. A year after this interview, done in 1994, both Marie and Henry died within days of each other. He was 100 and she was 96.

I was born up in the Aleutians on an island called Unga. My father had charge of three codfish stations and dories that fished for codfish. He had left Sweden when he was 14 and sailed around the world. Since he was on an English ship, he had to learn the English language. He learned the swear words first, he said. When he was 18 or 19 he came to San Francisco and sailed up to Unalaska. It was the same kind of country he had come from in Sweden so he decided to stay up there.

After time went by, he looked for someone to marry. He picked my mother out of the school. Her family had died of a flu epidemic and she was an orphan in the Methodist orphanage. Her name was Ludmelia Anna Prokopieff before she became an Anderson. My father's name was Carl John Anderson; he was a lot older than Mama.

I had a sister that was born first and then me, and then my brother Charlie, three years younger than me. My sister passed away when she was three. We stayed up there until I was going on seven. There was a schoolhouse but they couldn't get a teacher. Somebody said that down in Ketchikan there were not just one but two schools, a native school and a town school. So we sailed to San Francisco on a three-masted codfish schooner, then came up by steamboat to Ketchikan in 1905 or 1906.

Marie Henn

My dad sent some money to a friend in Ketchikan to buy a cabin. It was right across from where Paul Hansen's store used to be, straight up all those steps. But my dad wanted a place for a rowboat so he could get out and fish. Besides he didn't like shoveling off all those steps. We had lots of snow in those days.

So we finally got the place out here [near the present Lutheran Church] about 1907 or 1908. There were lots of trees around, and for a long time you couldn't get me off the boardwalk—I thought a bear would get me. Well, in Unga we didn't have trees, just rolling hills and lots of wind.

In those days we lived off the country. Salmon was plentiful. Dad would salt salmon bellies and put 'em in barrels, and then, too, we had salted deer meat. That's the only way you could take care of the deer unless you hung it up and dried it and things didn't dry so good here. We ate a lot of deer ribs and sauerkraut—boy, was that good—and it was my job to see that the food was out getting soaked for the next meal.

In the summertime we had a garden. In Sweden they raised kale and we had lots of kale. It lasted all winter. And we picked goose tongue on the beach. Charlie and I, we never objected to picking 'em 'cause we liked to eat 'em. Mama would get some salted ham hocks and cook 'em with a big pot of that goose tongue. But it took a lot of goose tongue 'cause they wilted down to hardly nothing. We had to pick them clean and wash them. But, gee whiz, them was good eatin'.

Once in awhile I would take care of some kids in the evening and sometimes they would give me an apple or an orange and sometimes 10 or 15 cents. If I got a banana, I would bring it home and divide it with Charlie and he would wash the dishes for me.

I would bring the money home and Mama would put it in my little pig bank. When I got that pig full I had over five dollars and I thought, "Boy, am I ever rich." Mama went and put it in the bank. I couldn't use it. That's how I got my bank account.

I had to use it for shoes. At Easter we always had new pairs of shoes. We couldn't wear them until that day. Sometimes they were a little bit short and sometimes they were not wide enough but we wore them.

Mama worked for different women when they had babies and sometimes she got paid and sometimes she didn't. Sometimes she just got sacks of old clothes. She would bring 'em home and I'd rip 'em up, wash 'em and remake 'em. I'd make my own clothes; that's how I learned to sew.

Charlie was lucky. He could sell papers to make money and buy stuff for himself. He wouldn't buy nothing for me, but he would buy Mama little things he thought she would like. So he always had good clothes, enough clothes.

The school was at the top of the hill where the Catholic Church used to be on Main Street. There was a girls' basement and a boys' basement, and they were separated by a rail. And then we had a hall where you could play basketball. We played tag and "jump-the-rail," too.

I was going on seven when I started school. Mama had taught me my ABCs and I could write my name and count. Reading was my main thing. I liked to read. I used to go to the library and just pick out books at random. If I didn't know the words, I looked them up in the dictionary.

We didn't use much store stuff. My dad worked in the summer and when he'd get through working, he'd buy a couple sacks of flour and a bunch of rice and cans of lard and junk like that, so we didn't need the store. We had our flour and we made bread every week.

We used to pick cranberries and dry them. Cranberry sauce was our main extra stuff in the winter. We didn't have much variety. We put up blueberries, and we ate a lot of clams.

My dad had a beard and he was always an old man to me. He was 20 years older than my mama was. She was gone a lot when women had babies, so he chopped wood and kept the house warm and he was a good cook. But he had a spittoon and Mama would get mad 'cause he'd spit in the fire and put it out.

Mama finally got steady work in the laundry doing fancy ironing for the red-light district girls. They had beautiful negligees that had to be hand-washed and hand-ironed. There were also stiff collars brought in by the men. Then the town was growing and the business grew big. They were getting more laundry off the steamers, too, because they did it cheaper and cleaner than Seattle. So they decided they were gonna have an office and needed somebody who did a little arithmetic. And I was lucky I had studied arithmetic; gee whiz, I was good at arithmetic. So I got that job. I had to keep track of each girl, how many hours; there was a special ironer who got more money and the girl who did nothing but collars and cuffs got more money. I think I got a dollar and a half a day but I had to pay room and board so I didn't have much spending money.

The driver picked up the laundry from the red-light girls and took it back, and they paid him. But there were a couple of the girls that wanted to have charge accounts so that was the only time they would ever come in. And when they came in, they were not painted or anything. They looked just like you or me.

And then Henry came along. He was from San Francisco and he worked on a lighthouse tender that docked at Talbot's dock and Charlie was working as a mess boy. And he brought Henry home with him to meet my dad 'cause my dad when he came from Sweden had landed in San Francisco. But Charlie didn't tell Henry that he had an older sister.

And I was home there with a friend at my house. She brought a cup of sugar over and I had a cup of sugar and we made taffy and pulled it, and that's what we were doing when Henry came along. Pulling taffy.

Henry came back to visit my dad and they talked about San Francisco. He didn't come back to visit me. But then one day he asked Mama if he could take me to the show at the Dream. He had a payday. "Yeah," Mama said, "but you have to be home right after the show." The show ended at 9:30. And we were, we ran home. So that's how I got to be acquainted with Henry.

Later Henry was working at Yes Bay and he came in and said, "Let's get married." "Well," I said, "I'm working." "Well," he said, "take one to two o'clock off and we can go up and get the license." Which we did. I told Mama I thought we'd get married. She said, "You have Henry get a minister and bring him to the house." Well, golly, Henry had his best man, his friend Lloyd White, come up and get the Methodist minister. We got married the 22nd of March, 1920, a cold rainy night. And he didn't take me out. I had to take him upstairs to my bedroom. We didn't have any money either. He lay around. We always laugh about that—he had to stay with me.

Then he went out to Yes Bay and I didn't see him until the end of the summer. Then he took me down to visit with his folks in San Francisco. (We were down there seven years.) They said we could stay with them, but Henry would have to go to work. I was scared to death of San Francisco, all those people and all them houses. 'Course Henry's folks lived up on 22nd Street up on the high hill. They were wealthy people. So I stayed home and helped his mother keep house.

Finally Henry got a job at the Globe Milling Company and we started getting money so we went out in the country and bought a piece of land with a tree on it. Then we had a one-room cabin built. It was all right, too, 'cause we lived outdoors under the tree most of the time anyway. We didn't need much.

We lived a block off the main highway. And we started raising chickens and selling eggs, so we had a good egg route. We had a garden and we planted fruit trees. My dad would come down in the winter and stay with us. Mama had passed away.

I had braids wound around my head and it was so hot that I had my hair cut off. Henry said, "You look good that way, you look comfortable." But his Uncle Jules and Aunt Pearl said, "You shouldn't have had your hair cut. Lettin' it grow that long and then gettin' rid of it. Only fast, sporty girls do that." And you know before the month was out, Aunt Pearl had her hair cut. Uncle Jules had a fit too. But after that she said, "Why, I should have had that done years ago." Oh, golly.

Henry and my dad and Uncle Jules came up to Ketchikan. And when Henry got back [to California] he said, "We're going to sell this place and go back." So that's how we got back up here and we've been here ever since. Oh, we've traveled around. We'd go out every winter and travel down to Key West. We saved our money and bought a car in Detroit. We drove up to Maine and worked our way down to Key West, then over to San Francisco. Henry would have to stop and get a job, or else I would. We had some money comin' in— we were renting our place in Ketchikan for $15 a month. We used that for spending money and ate carefully. I don't know how we did it, but we saw a lot of the country.

62

We own land out south of town. It was at the end of the road when we homesteaded it. You had to clear the land and live on it for three years and pay only $10 for it. We have beachfront property. We still go out there. I go for a few days at a time to clean it but Henry keeps the outside windows washed and things picked up. He likes to fish but what he likes best is to chop wood. When a drift log comes along he brings it in and cuts it up. There used to be trees blown down on the road and he always had to have his crosscut saw with us to clear the road.

But now the road goes past our land and there are houses. There's too many houses, too many sewers. So you can't get goose tongue on our beach anymore. And you can't just go across the bay and get them anymore either. That's all changed.

But, oh golly, such is life.

Ralph "Scooty" Homan

So don't try eatin' a blue jay.

Scooty Homan's father came to Ketchikan and worked for two or three years before he was able to send for Scooty, his mother and older brother in June of 1919. Within a few years the Homans built a home, joining the group of Norwegian families who settled along what is now Tongass Avenue. Scooty has been an outdoor person all his life.

I went to Charcoal Point School, which used to be Dynamite Joe's old roadhouse. The government came in during prohibition and took it away from him—Dynamite Joe was selling booze, ya know. Boy! That was quite a trade in those years. I can remember these boats would come from Rupert and bring up the liquor to Ketchikan. They were painted black. And they had—I saw one—two Rolls Royce engines and they could do 50 knots. Our Coast Guard boats were down by Mary Island, and they were supposed to go out and intercept them. But those boats from Canada that came up with liquor, they just went right by. And Dynamite Joe, ya know, he was the worst!

In Charcoal Point School, we had three rooms and three teachers. All eight grades—each room had two or three grades. And you had to hear the same stories over for three years. They had wood stoves, and we went and got the wood and kept the stoves goin'. Just an old platform outside to play on. We put up a basket and played basketball, rain or shine. The school was there right where the ferry system is now. That beach between there and Sunny Point was tide flats and we took all the rocks off at low tide and we played baseball at low tide. We only had one ball, and if you knocked the ball into the bay, you had to go out and get it.

Ralph "Scooty" Homan

We played baseball, we played basketball, we went trout fishing, we went hunting, rain or shine. And we didn't mind the rain, just put on different gear for different occasions. Kids who were born and raised here are adaptable to anything there is. It's the kind of country we live in.

There was an oldtimer lived in a little house right across the street from the school. He was a gunsmith and his name was Chris—that's all I knew. He was very patient with us school kids. When I got my first gun at six, it didn't have a sight on it. He put a front sight on it and sighted that thing in. Boy, did he sight it in. I asked him how much and he said, "Have you got a dollar?" Well, I had two dollars in my pocket, but he did it for a dollar and he worked a lot of time on it. Anyhow, his place burned down. And it wasn't two weeks later he had a house that was much nicer than the one that burned down. Everybody at Charcoal Point helped him rebuild.

That first gun was a little .22 long-barrel thing. I could shoot a berry off a bush. I shot my first deer when I was nine on top of Bear Mountain. We went out and got ducks and geese and deer and, 'course, fish. I had a little route where I went out and caught red snapper, halibut, even rock cod, and on Friday I would sell them to the Catholic people. I'd get two bits for a couple of fish.

In the winter, I would go with the neighbor kids—Bill, Ben, and Maud Raleigh—over to Gravina Island, skating at Long Lake and Pond Lake. There'd be a big gang of us and we'd build a big fire. The first boat would break the ice and the others would use the same path to get over there. In the summer we'd go over and go swimming. Maud would go with eight to 10 boys…and no bathing suits, which didn't bother Maud at all! She wore a suit, but we didn't.

I was 12 years old when John Peters—he was in his 60s—and I went hunting. We spent five weeks on the beach. Five weeks! We took off and it was a beautiful day, a westerly wind, we were going up Behm Canal. But you know how it can get, westerly wind. Water was comin' over the pilothouse, so he changed course and went across to Prince of Wales. His favorite spot was Polk Inlet, just past Kasaan Bay. You go way up in the inlet, good hunting country. So we anchored up there for the first day hunting. We were clear up

66

on top of the hill and I heard him shoot. I went up there, and he had a beautiful, big four-point buck. I wasn't much for packin' a four-pointer and we mostly dragged it down the hill. The wind started blowin', and I mean it blew. And pretty soon twigs and hunks of branches were flyin' around. We got down to the beach and . . . no boat!

It was blowin' and rainin' and gettin' dark. So we huddled underneath this cedar tree. We both lay next to the deer—it was still warm—but that was a miserable night. At the crack of dawn, we went to look for the boat. I got in the little punt we'd rowed ashore in, and rowed down the bay, lookin'. And I found the boat—it had drug and gone on a rock and tipped over and sunk. You could see part of the mast was sticking up. I think when it went on the rock and laid on its side, part of it was burned, too. 'Course there we were. It was getting into November and getting cold. But we lived off the land. That's the time I ate seagulls, I ate crows. We ate everything. We took the deer, sliced it up, built a fire and smoked it.

I sure learned a lot about living off the land with old John. He was no slouch. All we had in the punt was a three-pound coffee can for bailing—that became our cook pot. There was a little creek and we put rocks across it and had a nice little hole for washing ourselves. We made a lean-to. He had me getting skunk cabbage leaves. We laid those and made kind of a roof. As time went on, we had a pretty fair place.

Then I shot a second deer, too. A doe came out on the flats and I got that. That way we both had a blanket instead of using just one old deerskin. That was a good place to survive 'cause there were lots of clams and mussels. He told me we should eat some berries. Well, berries were about gone that time of the year, but salal berries still grow late in the fall and we ate a lot of those. And wild cranberries, they're sour as heck, but I ate 'em.

John liked those black mussels. I'd gather up bunches of them. And he'd throw those clams and mussels in the red-hot coals, they'd pop, and he really liked those things. John was busy all the time doin' things like makin' mittens out of deer hide.

I trapped these seagulls. I had a log, a flat log, and I made a little trigger to put clams on, and the seagulls would go to bite the clam, and this log would fall on them. Might not kill 'em, but then

I'd run down and wring their necks. So we'd have a seagull. But there's not much to a seagull, mostly feathers, but good when you're hungry. But I tell you one bird I won't eat, even if I'm starving. I got one of them too—a blue jay. Oh, rancid-tasting thing! Holy smoke! It tasted like poison. So don't try eatin' a blue jay.

After five weeks went by we heard a *put-put-put* and here comes this little boat up the bay. He stopped down there and he rowed ashore. His name was Blackie—that's all I know. Just a pot of a boat with a two-cylinder engine in it. He was setting traps, big traps, along the shore there. So he came in and got us.

My family couldn't believe it, you know, when we made it home. They had searched every bay and inlet in Behm Canal and had more or less given us up.

But I'd like to go back to Polk Inlet sometime and see that old cedar tree. It was a great big cedar tree. It kept us out of the wind and gave pretty good coverage. We had a good camp there.

One time, a few days before Thanksgiving, my brother and I rowed over to Gravina, hoping to get some ducks or geese for Thanksgiving dinner. And my brother had a 12-gauge shotgun, single shot, and I had a smaller one, a 20-gauge single shot, 'cause I was much smaller. We were rowing over there and here coming down the channel were two lone geese. All of a sudden they circled around and they landed down there at Government Creek, where the airport is now. So we rowed in and we crawled up there and we could hear them behind the rocks, they were cackling, so I raised up slow—I could see one—I took careful aim and bang! I got it. The other one flew up and went over my brother and he shot it on the fly. So we got these two geese. But that part wasn't so remarkable. They weren't Canadian honkers—the kind of geese we have around here. They were brown geese with orange feet, what they call a "Ross" goose. They're not found in this area, so we always say that the Good Lord sent 'em to us for Thanksgiving. They were delicious. I don't know what they'd been feeding on, must have been wild cranberries or something, because they were one of the best feeding birds I've had.

Of course, my mother was Norwegian and an excellent cook. Thanksgiving and holidays, oldtimers would come to our house for dinner. It was just a ritual. And Sundays—we went to church every Sunday and my mother left the coffeepot on the back of the stove and the table all set. She'd have homemade bread and all kinds of stuff, and when we were at church lots of oldtimers came to our house and helped themselves. That's just the way things worked. I didn't come home from church any Sunday that somebody hadn't been to our house and had something to eat.

After I graduated in '37, I went right aboard the *Cedar* in the Lighthouse Service. I was a mess boy the first year, then I went on and got to be officers' mess, $75 a month. Then I got to be a fireman. We'd be gone for four months, doing all the lights and buoys, all the way to the Pribilof Islands. I put in two years and got enough to buy a boat.

I bought the hull from the Nakat Packing Cannery up at the head of Cholmondeley. It had a 12-horse heavy-duty Atlas and was designed something like a double-ender. So I had the Raleighs—they were real good boat-builders—take off all the old planks and build this trolling boat with a trunk cabin and lots of room for packin' fish. The galley wasn't much—had a table and a couple bunks. That boat was under water more than it was on top, but that's the reason I'm here now, on account of the way that boat was built. It was built solid.

I was fishin' around Noyes Island and I'd go into Craig for gas and supplies. And that's where I met Irene. I fell for her like a ton of bricks. She was a beauty. Blond hair, Norwegian, beautiful complexion. She was divorced and had two little girls. Anyhow, we got to the point where things were getting serious. I took my boat to Ketchikan and packed up my few belongings and I was going to Craig to get married. I said good-bye to the family and my dad said, "Hey, are you sure you want to do this?" And I said, "Oh, yeah, I can't live here forever." And he said, "Well, you're always welcome."

So I took off early in the morning and it was blowing a little bit and it was too rough to go south, so I was goin' around the north end. I got as far as Ship Island, maybe 20 miles from town, right out in the middle of the channel and by that time it was gettin' pretty rough, and the engine blew the head.

There I was, out in the middle of the straits. The boat was rollin' around, and I was drifting toward Prince of Wales, that narrow point. It was gettin' dark and I could hear the waves and knew I was goin' to go on the beach.

But during those years we used a little sail as a stabilizer. It kept you steady when it was rough. So I went out and raised up that little sail and I tacked off shore that night. And I went in the wheel-house to turn the thing, and the boat took a roll and I went headfirst on top of the engine. Just about knocked myself out; I had a big lump on my head. I sailed all that night and all the next day and I got up to Snow Pass. There's an island there called Bushy Island and there was a fox farm there. So I put over my punt and towed the boat into that harbor, dropped the anchor and went ashore.

There was a fellow and his sister who owned the fox farm. At breakfast the next morning, she says, "Well, we'd like to hire you." It was pelting season, and so I said, "Hey, if I can eat here, well, that's great!"

They had feeding stations all around the island. They had a system there where the fox would go in to feed and the door would come down so they were captured in this little feeding-house. So we went out. She had these tongs and she'd get 'em and she'd put 'em in a sack, and we'd walk back. And she couldn't stand the thought of killing 'em, 'cause some of those little foxes she used to feed with bottles. Her brother had to do all the dirty work—pelting and stuff.

So this went on for over a week. 'Course there wasn't much boat traffic. Finally, a little boat came in there from Wrangell. My family didn't know if I was alive or dead. So I wrote this letter to my brother and told him where I was and everything. So he went to the Coast Guard and told 'em about it. 'Course the Coast Guard was entirely different then than now. They used to lay at the float for months and not even move. So they told my brother, "He's probably layin' in the harbor drunk or something." At that time of my life (I was 21) I'd never even tasted a drink!

Anyhow, nothin' happened. Three weeks later late at night I heard an old diesel engine—*kachicka, kachicka, kachicka.* So I rowed out in the channel and waved a flashlight. John Munson came in and

I told him my situation and he towed me to town. So I was over three weeks late for my own wedding!

After we were married [in 1940] I put in about six years of fishing. In 1942, I was trolling off Cape Addington in about 50 fathoms. And during the war we were all scared of the Japs. That night I was the last boat out and it was gettin' dusk. I started to pull my poles and go in. I saw a small little boat on the outside and he was just driftin'. I turned around to assist him, you know, and this Japanese submarine pulled up on the outside of him. I started goin' toward shore. I looked back and the little boat was already headin' in, so I wasn't worried about him.

I wasn't the only who saw all this, 'cause the next morning the fish buyers—the Knaplunds with the *Beloit II*—they had a radio and called in. And the planes from Annette Island, the bombers, went out and I think they crippled the sub.

Then the old *Foremost*, she was a halibut schooner converted to a Coast Guard boat with depth charges on her. But when her crew dropped the charges, they were so slow they did some damage to themselves. They couldn't get away from the charges fast enough.

During those years I fished halibut in the spring, trolled all summer and in the winter I fished black cod and shark. Gee, I had muscles on me you couldn't believe!

But my last trip . . . I left Muzon with a full load of cohos right up to the hatch. And I was talking with a fisherman there, I said, "How does the weather look?" 'Course you had no communications then, you had nothin'. So he said, "Mmm, it looks O.K." I got halfway across when the storm hit. So help me, it was 20-25-foot swells. Going around Chacon the boat was under water more than it was on top. I'd go clear under and see the water up above. I looked back for my skiff, and it was gone. Everything was gone. Water kept comin' up into the engine; it was partway up in the engine. I finally got around the cape there and into McLean's Arm. And I had to throw all the fish out of the middle there 'cause the bilge pump didn't work. And I could see why—it had screen around and it was full of scales— just solid. So I got that all cleaned out and pumped the boat out and, boy, I tell ya, I was eight hours off of Chacon in that sea!

Well, when I got to town there wasn't a trollin' pole on her, runnin' lights, nothin'. That boat was stripped clean. And I says, "Lord, this is my last trip." I fixed the boat up and sold it. I says, "I got a family to take care of. I can't try this again."

Because Irene and I had the two little ones, you know.

And now we have nine grandchildren and 10 great-grand-children. And all but three are still in Ketchikan. And, same as the rest of us, they don't mind the rain.

The weather never bothered me. Been here too long, I guess. But, hey, if I wanted to go hunting or fishing or anything, I'd put on my rain gear and go. And I can look across at every one of those mountains on Gravina and I've been on every one of them. Every single one.

Merta Kiffer

I would say I am a real sourdough.

Born and raised in Ketchikan, Merta Kiffer has lived through the Depression, the war years and the arrival of Statehood. In turn she also raised a family, on a homesite at Clover Pass, and still finds Southeast Alaska a good place to live.

I would say I am a real sourdough because I was born in a small house on the banks of Ketchikan Creek. I think my mother's father and mother, the Harts, came here first around 1910. My grandfather was somewhat of a prospector and he also was Chief of Police here for a short time back in the early days. His wife, my grandmother, was a practical nurse.

My father's parents were Smiths. First two older sons Harry and James and later their parents came. Harry eventually started Smith Electric and my grandfather eventually started Smith's Plumbing and Sheet Metal for which my dad and my Uncle Hobart worked. To begin with, my dad worked for Citizens' Light and Power, the company that is now Ketchikan Public Utilities. My Uncle Hobart did also and my mother worked at one time as a telephone operator there. (Many years later I worked there myself.)

There were prospectors on both sides of the family. Grandfather Smith, when he left Chicago after he and my grandmother were first married, had some mining claims in Washington State. My grandfather Hart had some mining claims at Niblack on Prince of Wales Island and I think they also lived at Dolomi at one time. They also lived up at the old Schoenbar Mine. It was not running at that time and I think Grandfather acted as somewhat of a watchman. My mother used to talk about walking down the trail to school, which was on Main Street then, and hearing the wolves howling.

Merta Kiffer

I was born in the '20s. My first memory is living in the little house on what is now Freeman Street, wading in the creek and riding in the shop truck with my dad. There wasn't anything beyond the ball park. Across from it there were some houses on Park Avenue but nothing on Deermount above the "Y" at Woodland and Deermount. Deermount was called Mahoney Heights.

When I started school we were living in what we called the red house near the foot of Austin. Tongass Avenue was a wide board street at that time on pilings and so the tide came right into our front yard.

We moved to the "West End" because my dad's family business had subcontracted work on White Cliff School, which they were finishing about then. I think my dad made the sign for White Cliff School, among other things. When I was between seven and eight my parents bought a house at the top of Austin Street. Austin was a board street at that time.

I like to say I am a charter member of White Cliff. I opened the school in the first grade, my classmates and I. And I went there from the first grade through the sixth and then had to go down to Main School for the seventh and eighth and high school. My first grade teacher Miss McFarland was a really good teacher and all the children liked her. Some of us did so well under her tutelage that we skipped third grade.

Reading has been my favorite subject. It was just like a new world when I learned to read. I think children were more inclined to read then because that was what there was to do when you were stuck inside. Our backyard was the woods and we used to like to play in the woods a lot, too.

Then I went to Main School for seventh through high school. I can remember sitting in civics class looking over at the courthouse which was across the street at the time, the courthouse and the jail. The high school was on the upper floor, separated from the junior high and the grades.

For fun we went to the Peter Pan. It was an ice cream parlor and you could buy sandwiches. Sometimes we went there for lunch if we had the money. You could walk down the hill and you would be at the Peter Pan. It was a nice big place run by a couple of sisters. The hamburger with a bun was not "in" yet.

Downtown there was Heckmans, the Bon Marche and Tongass Trading, which had a grocery section then. There was Hunt's Bookstore and several grocery stores. There was the Stedman Hotel and Café. And there was the Champion Shoe Store in the Red Men Building. When I was young we had two or three theaters. Unfortunately with progress we have but one.

I liked Thompson and Hattrick's, a clothing store, and a little dress shop owned by a woman named Jeanette across Edmonds [Street] from the Daily News. I think our family also went to Sears a lot.

Our high school class was about the biggest up until then. There were forty-some in it, I think. We had two home rooms. We would all meet in the auditorium first and we had sing-alongs. Sometimes a different class would entertain. When our freshman class had to entertain, some of us did a square dance on the stage.

There was a statue of Diana the Huntress on the wall of the auditorium some feet up and every year the freshman class would try to decorate it. We all put clothing on it, signs or whatever. But one year and I think it was some people in our class stole the banner of one of the upper classes and hid it, and the class was pretty upset. Decorating Diana was already a custom when we came along.

When we were living at the top of Austin, some of the men got together and built a kind of a high line up to this cliff. They would cut wood up there and then send the blocks down on the cable to the foot there at the top of Austin where they would retrieve them. Most of us in the early days had wood stoves. Our furnace was wood to begin with. Father did put oil in eventually. Being a sheet metal worker, he built our furnaces. And when we lived up on what is now Freeman Street, they were starting to get bathrooms indoors. Anyway we didn't have a bathtub in the little house so my dad built one out of sheet metal. He built cupboards and coolers out of sheet metal too instead of out of wood.

You didn't have your supermarkets then. There were lots of small grocery stores in the West End. One big difference was that meat markets were separate. At the grocer's you didn't buy your meat, you bought canned goods, produce and staples. You went to the counter and the clerk waited on you or else you phoned in your order and they delivered it.

I worked one summer at the Ward Cove Cannery when I was about 15. I really enjoyed it. There were a lot of young people working there. The town was full of canneries. The smell of fish hung pretty heavily in the summer. It wasn't a rotten smell but a kind of cooked fish smell.

I did quite a bit of babysitting, too. And I worked in the hospital kitchen one summer and then in the fall I went to work for the telephone company as an apprentice operator. That was an interesting job. I worked for them for about a year. Then I got married and quit and we went trapping.

My husband's folks had a boat too, and we went out together over on Prince of Wales and we trapped there until around Christmas and then we came in. And I think after that we trapped a little in Cholmondeley and then south in George Inlet for a short bit. My mother-in-law, Gladys, and I had a good time there.

One time we were in Polk Inlet and my husband Kenny and his dad were out in the skiff and outboard running the trap lines. It was mostly beach trapping for mink and occasionally an otter. Gladys suggested we get in the small punt and row ashore in the harbor and look at the traps. We found a mink in one or two and took them out. When the men came back they were quite upset. Somebody had been stealing their mink! Naturally they discovered they were mistaken but it was amusing at the time. I enjoyed it out there and I had my mother-in-law for company while the men were out on the trap line, so that helped.

My husband was good at fishing and hunting so we always had plenty of those things on hand to eat. When the weather was good it was nice tramping in the woods, hunting. But I think I always preferred to go trout fishing. At least you knew where you were going, you got there and you fished. With the hunting you could go all over. We usually came back with a deer. I never shot any but Kenny did and my mother-in-law shot a few deer in her life.

77

We had been renting in town and had our first son Ken, or Jimmy as he was called then, and Kenny thought he would like to get a place out in the country that had a stream for water and not a bad harbor for the boat. We found a place near where the Clover Pass Resort is now so we made arrangements and homesited there. Mr. Hodgman [from the U.S. Forest Service] came out and surveyed it for us and Kenny's folks had decided to move out too, so they took up the place alongside us. At that time there wasn't anything much there where the resort is now.

We started clearing that fall and then went up to Loring. Kenny bought a cannery building there. It was the office building and store. He bought it for $25. We got enough lumber for both houses—for us and for his folks. It was good fir lumber, a real buy. So we went up there and stayed a month or so and tore it down. The front pilings were gone and it was slanted with the front end down floating in the water so it was kind of exciting being in it, but the men tore it down and Gladys and I pulled nails like mad.

We rafted it up and we even got some flue blocks out of it for the chimney. We towed it down to where we were going to build the houses. We got logs for the piling for under the houses, the foundation, and we had to buy maybe a few rafters or joists. It had what they called at that time "beaded" ceilings and walls. We put masonite in the kitchen and painted it and papered it with felt paper for the living room.

It was the fall of 1941 that we tore down the building at Loring and then we started building the houses [at Clover Pass]. They weren't finished by far, the outside had tar paper and the inside partitions weren't all quite finished, but we moved in and stayed there that winter. We didn't have any plumbing, but we had each bought a small light plant, so we had electricity of sorts and we had bathrooms inside. The men built a dam on the creek behind us and put a water line down, which went to the two houses. But for the first year, I remember, we had a water barrel on the little back porch there.

Homesiting was quite different from homesteading. You didn't have to clear all that land for one thing. You had to clear enough to build a house and you had to live in it for I think it was five years. We paid a very small sum every year to the Forest Service for it and then when you were ready, you had this plat made and posted. You had to apply to Congress and then I think you paid so much per acre to the Bureau of Public Lands.

After we had lived there for some years, some cousins of Kenny's folks bought Hansen's place on the point where the resort is now and another family moved out there and had children so we got enough for a school. The North Point Higgins road was built which was a real bonanza, so we no longer had to walk a trail up to the highway or row around Knudson Cove.

The state said if we provided the school, they would provide a teacher, but we had to find her a place to live. The men got together and built a small school. It was just a small one-room school with an outhouse in the back. They found a house for the teacher to rent and we had our first school there. The children at least didn't have to hike to the highway and take that long bus ride into town early in the morning.

There was a bus service at that time. Old Wacker sold out his bus line in town and started one out the road and I think it went to the end of the road and back. It didn't go every day, but that bus was really nice. Quite a lot of us used it. It was a lot of fun. You would see everybody getting on and off and go on their way. People you knew or people you just knew by sight. We didn't get into town more than once a week. You could go in and do your shopping, visit and what-ever, and then go back later in the day.

I was lucky that my husband wasn't called up during the war because he was a fisherman and had a food production deferment. And of course, we had a family. We had two children by then. By the end of it we had a third son. Right at the end of the war he would have had to go but I think the atomic bomb came in time to prevent that. We definitely knew there was a war on and it was always a worry that you would hear somebody you knew was killed or injured because there were a lot of them away.

Well, much has changed. We kinda hoped after the war we were going to get Statehood, but we didn't and it took another 10 years or so. Of course the cannery interests fought it strongly and

79

they had a good lobby in Washington. I think a lot of people wanted Statehood, but there were those who said we can't afford it. It seems that we could, and I think the one reason, because of the oil, that Congress decided and the powers that be, that we could afford it. It has been a mixed blessing since they still want to run everything from Washington D.C.

I thought of moving south after my husband died. I had three sisters and my mother down in the Seattle area, but I looked it over and saw what it was like. If you didn't drive and have a car you were dependent on others to help you. Here, you can be more independent. You can walk or get to the doctor or dentist or whatever. It is more of a laid-back, slower pace here.

I like the water and the mountains. I am so used to them by now. I am not sure I would be happy inland—where it's flat with no ocean. I think life here is pretty good. It has been for me. I have been very fortunate.

Herman Ludwigsen

Flying is my life. Got to be.

The son of Nels and Amaile Ludwigsen, Herman was born into a family famous for its boat building skills. But since high school days Herman Ludwigsen has been hitched to the skies. He met and married his wife Anita in Bethel in 1953 and their first child was born in Ketchikan. They returned for a time to Bethel where two more children were born.

My dad was a boat-builder and a ship's carpenter in the Puget Sound area for a long time. We lived in a boathouse in Seattle down by the government locks. In 1935 or '36 he started building his own boat, a 36-foot troller. Finally he got tired of Seattle. We were dead poor, practically living on the bread line. It was during the Depression time. Nine of us got on the damn little 36-footer and followed two other trollers up here to Alaska. We had one hell of a boat ride to Alaska. All of us seasick. It was tough. We'd stop in a harbor and lay over for the night and travel again. It took us about a week. Tough ride. We arrived in Ketchikan in the spring of '38.

During those years I went to White Cliff School. That was when I got indoctrinated into airplanes. Herb Munter had his own airline right down below our house. I used to see these little airplanes flying around all the time and thought, "God, I would love to do that!" There was a guy named Jimmy Reinhart. He was down at Herb Munter's hangar. And he had a little J2 Cub on wooden floats, wooden prop, 45-horse engine. He took me for a ride. That was about '39 or '40. We circled over White Cliff School and flew around a little bit, and then went down and landed. That was all it took! After that, in the evenings I would go down to the hangar and help wash airplanes, wash windshields. I

Herman Ludwigsen

got free rides once in awhile over to Annette Island when they were building the airport.

Besides airplanes, while growing up in Ketchikan I remember the holidays and special events. Like the Fourth of July, when everybody would head for Black Sands Beach. That was in the late '30s and the '40s. The canneries and everything would shut down and we'd all get on these barges and fish scows. That was the Eagles picnic. They would furnish hot-dogs, pop, hell everything was free. Big time with lots of people, lots of fun. We had foot races and swimming races and horseshoes, a typical '40s mentality. Nobody was in a hurry; it was just a laid-back type thing and everybody had a few beers.

In them days the Fourth of July was the Fourth of July. They shut down Dock Street. They had a big sawdust pile for the kids to find money by digging around in it. There were boxing matches at the ballpark. In the water there were seine boat races, and tug boat tug-o-wars, trolling boat races and log rolling contests. Everybody was seeing if they could beat each other. There was a nice parade. It was a real good old-fashioned Fourth of July.

I can remember winters in the '40s. They'd shut down Main Street for sliding in the snow. We'd start way up on the hill by Revilla Apartments. Sleds, toboggans and all. Hell, everybody was sliding down that sucker. Then you would end up clear down at the spruce mill by old Bucey's garage. That was a lot of fun. That was when we had winters in Ketchikan. Ice froze across the bay. It froze clear across, but the ice wasn't thick enough to walk on. They had to have boats go out and break it up. There was a lot of people skating in Thomas Basin on the ice. We would also go over and ice skate on the lakes, row across the bay at night in the moon light and go over to Long Lake which we called it then. That is when people used to live on Gravina. There was always big parties back there on the ice.

I was about 11 or 12 when the war came. I can remember walking down the street when everybody said the war was declared. That same night, I don't know how in hell it happened but that evening the Deer Mountain cabin burnt down. It was a great big beautiful log cabin up on top of Deer Mountain. Some sucker went up there and burned it down and all the people in Ketchikan including the Coast

83

Guard thought that it was a signal to the Japanese to move in. It was serious business there for awhile.

It was tough to even move in the harbor during the war. The Navy set up this tower at Ryus Float. Any boat that wanted to move had to go to the tower and have someone stand on deck and holler to the guy on the tower, where you were going, who you were and what your business was. Every boat had to do that in the harbor.

During the war there were Canadians in the air from Annette Island. They had bombers. They would come over to Ketchikan and would practice air raids, and they would drop flour bags on us. Everybody in the school would run like hell out of the way because we were being bombed by the Japanese supposedly. It was the Canadian bombers and they were crazy! Them buggers were nuts! I've seen some crazy pilots in my day, but those guys! I mean, these big twin-engine bombers were less than treetop altitude, buzzing everything and dropping these goddamn flour sacks on everybody.

I fished with my brother and my dad every day when I was a little guy. Fished on their trollers, went out fishing all summer long; I didn't have time to play softball or baseball like the other kids, until I got into high school. I did a lot of rowing, going down to the old cold storage when San Juan Jack was there. They had a fish buying station. They all loved to hire me because I was cheap. I would unload halibut boats when the oldtimers didn't want to get down there in the slime. They would give me a fish to take home and a little bit of money. Also, all the oldtimers were there fishing herring right out in front of the cold storage dock. In fact they would tag off the cold storage dock and make a hook of it and circle right there and come back in with a boatload of herring. I would help unload those. I stunk so bad. I was a young husky fellow, and I was energetic. When I would go home in the evening after all that my mom would have to hold her nose I stunk so bad. I can remember she would run the bath water. The bathroom and bathtub weren't in the house. We had to go out of the house and into a shed where the bathroom was. She would run the water in the bathtub and poured Lysol in the tub to get the stink off of me.

The work, unloading boats and what not, it was just sort of

pickup work. Just to have some money because things weren't great. We were a big family and like anybody else we lived on deer meat and fish in them days, and whatever else you could get. I would fish all summer and go to school in the winter.

In high school, we played basketball, we didn't call ourselves the Kayhi Kings then, we called ourselves the Kayhi Polar Bears. I started my freshman year. I was good enough to be on the second string. We traveled around to Petersburg, Metlakatla and Prince Rupert. I did earn a stripe my freshman year, which was unheard of for a freshman to earn a stripe as a varsity player. Some of the other older fellows were a little bit upset because I had earned a stripe and the "K" that you could sew on your sweater. The letter, year, the stripe goes with it. In my sophomore year I proved that some of them weren't as good as me. From then on I was on first string. I played basketball real hard. I won a lot of trophies and sportsmanship awards and allstar trophies. I really loved basketball.

Our coach and some of the teachers would transport us to games. The coach, old Mr. Hanna, we used to travel in his yacht. He'd pile all us kids on that damn boat and we'd go to Petersburg, Wrangell, all the way to Juneau. Once we got stuck and had to anchor up in Taku Harbor and wait for the wind to calm down. We'd all share the cooking and chores. That was with Victor Klose, Gus Olsen, Bob Crowder, Leif Leding and, gee, there was a whole bunch of us young guys. We had a good ball team. We won All-State twice.

I didn't graduate, though. When you get to be as smart as I was in them days you are smarter than the teachers and you knew more than they did. One of the teachers, it was in a civics class or something, I was foolin' around in back there not being my normal self. She stood me up in front of class and said, "What did you come to school for?" I said, "To play basketball." She said, "Get out!" Out the door I went and I never came back. I had been fishing every year with my dad and making money, so he bought me a troller.

Before that, in my sophomore year, 1945, Jim Webber started a flying school, him and Dr. McKenzie. They had four little Luscomb 65-horse airplanes. I was in love with airplanes anyway. So I would just go from school right down there across the dock and I would help gas airplanes and work for Jim Webber and Doc McKenzie.

They were training students and they had the GI flight-training program. Ralph Bartholomew and a few guys got their license. Finally Jim Webber took me for a ride in one and thought that I would be a pretty good pilot 'cause I took things seriously. So he took me out a few times.

A year later Pete Cessnun joined it. Pete had just got out of the service; he was a bomber pilot in England. So he came down to Webber and got a job as an instructor. After he came there, Don Ross showed up and he was a P-51 pilot in England, and then Hank Aegerter showed up and he was a P-47 pilot in Africa. There I was and all these guys had a part in training me to fly. I soloed in one of the quickest times they have ever had anybody solo. Four and one-half hours and they turned me loose in an airplane. In them days Webber was paying me $25.00 a week no matter how long you stayed there, from daylight to dark or real early in the morning. I got $25.00 a week for work and all the flying time I could steal. That was after the war, '45 to '47.

As I said, after I left school my father bought me a troller. We didn't fish much in the winter. There was winter fishing but I didn't do much of it, 'cause I would fly, go down to Webber all the time and get flying time and put in a lot of hours. So fishing during the summer and flying in the wintertime—I did that from late '47 until 1950. Then I got rescued. Uncle Sam called and I went into the army from '50-'52. Two years, drafted.

After I came back from the army, I tried to make a living flying. I was cheating on the government. That's normal for everybody anyhow. I didn't have a commercial license, but I had an airplane and knew a lot about hunting and fishing. I was taking guys out hunting, and fish-spotting for the fishermen like Dick Sanchez and Nels Nelson and all the boys. I would be way out at Chacon flying around spotting fish and talking to them on the radio. Makin' some money that way. It wasn't a lucrative business because there was a lot of fish and they didn't need too much from me anyway, but it helped some.

In the fall of '53, I was just married, gonna have a baby and living in the shack behind my dad's house. It was a real bad day and an oil millionaire named Ellis Hall was on Annette Island with his family and a bunch of other people. It was a day that even Ellis Airline wasn't flying the Grummans to the airport to pick people up off Pan Am and PNA. This Texas millionaire figured that he could beat it anyway. It didn't make any difference—if you got money you can go anywhere you like. So he took off under strict orders not to and headed for Smithers, B.C.

He didn't make it.

It was one of the biggest searches in Alaska history. It was a big search, over 30 days, Canadian and American Coast Guard, Navy, everybody locally. All nine pilots with airplanes came around and we formed a cooperative to help find this guy. Condor Oil Company was his company and they posted a $30,000 reward, plus they would pay for all of our gas and expenses for our airplanes if we would go out and look for this guy. There were nine of us guys and we couldn't find him. A month went by—30 days and nobody could find this guy. We crisscrossed everything. Everybody said to hell with it; we ain't going to find him; he must have gone in the water.

One day I loaded my airplane. I was headed for Quadra. I was going to go there and shoot ducks on the duck flats. I came around the corner at Porpoise Point just inside Quadra, right across from Mink Bay. I wasn't flying real high, and I saw something white down in the trees. I looked and, damn, that didn't look right so I made a big turn and come back, and there was the airplane. It was laying down there in the trees. I circled a bit more up a little higher and I saw a wing. Now, this wing was a greenish color, but it was right out in the open on the muskeg on that hillside. I don't see how nobody could miss it. You could make the wing out distinctively and you could see the great big ribs in the wings plain as day up there on the side of the hill. I circled around a little while trying to think that maybe I found the wrong thing—or the right thing. Finally I saw the rest of the fuselage in the trees. Then I started beatin' it out of there.

I called Dick Sanchez on the *Alamarie* and told him what I found. He congratulated me. I headed home to Webber Air. It was only 25 minutes to Ketchikan. I was going to tell them I had found the airplane. The news got there so damn fast, everybody was on the dock waiting for me to show up. They give me a check for $30,000. I took it down to the bank and I remember the banker was Bob

Buchanan, Oddy we called him. I showed him the check and the guy from Condor Petroleum was right behind me. Buchanan knew me. I was always broke anyway, he said, "What the hell is this, a joke?" I said, "I don't think so, ask this guy behind me." He said, "This is no joke, this is Herman's money, put it in the bank." So, I had a big dinner out at the Narrows [Supper Club] for all the pilots and their wives and I gave them each $1,000. I didn't have to. We didn't have any signed agreement or nothing, and we had quit. We abandoned our search effort. The other pilots thought that I should pay them anyway. So the wife and I talked about it a lot. We finally decided we would have a big dinner and give them each $1,000. We paid them off and paid Uncle Sam a hell of a pile, $6,000 or $7,000. There wasn't much left, I bought the wife silverware, a washer-dryer combination from Terry Myser. We spent the money foolishly, just like anybody else would.

I was good at airplanes. After the Ellis Hall wreck, I found a total of nine airplanes. The biggest find was when I was in Bethel flying, I found a downed Air Force C123 with 11 Air Force guys on it. I found the Bilderback airplane that crashed over at Karta, and a guy that crashed up in Downdraft Lake on Gravina.

I also rescued old man Sutherland out at Refuge Cove. He had sunk out at Channel Island in his skiff in rough water. I was going to Thorne Bay and looked down in the water, and damn, gas cans floating all over and junk in the water. I thought, "God, there is somebody in trouble." It was a bum day but I circled around and landed. There was old Sutherland hanging onto that damn gas can. Me and another guy got out of the airplane and drug him inside.

Every year I tell my wife, well, this is it. It's got to be my last year flying. But hell, if you can make it to 67 why not 70? If you're healthy enough and your mind is thinking clearly and you can fly the airplane and keep the people safe and pass your flight physical, why not? Why sit home and look out the window and every time you hear an airplane engine, run to the door to see who it is and wish it was you. I've been flying for 44 years now and it is all I know. Flying is my life, it's got to be until the end.

Got to be.

Conrad Mather

We're the bark people.

Born in Ketchikan in 1923, Conrad Mather takes pride in his Tsimshian heritage and is an energetic promoter of its language and culture. His mother was a girl when the missionary Father Duncan led the Tsimshians from "old" Metlakatla in Canada to "new" Metlakatla in Alaska.

I am Tsimshian Indian. I lived here during the Territorial days, during the '30s, known as the Depression years. My father Paul Mather was a priest at St. Elizabeth's Episcopal Church. I was just an altar boy. My parents were from Metlakatla. They moved to Ketchikan and built a house not far from the Salvation Army Hall. My father worked as a millwright in the Ketchikan Spruce Mill.

Mr. Leonard Allen was a white man from Michigan, and he was the principal of our Indian School, our grade school for Indians. We had three tribes at the school—Tlingit, Haida and Tsimshian. My sister was a teacher and my cousin was Mr. Allen's secretary. The school had a curio store too, and we made things like small totems and sold them to the tourists.

Mr. Allen was the first white man in the whole Territory to compile the Indian history of the Territory of Alaska. It was known as "Our Heritage." It was supposed to be a community affair, with all school families contributing, not sitting and writing like an anthropologist.

Well, the local Indians didn't know their culture. They had a tough time getting stories. But Chief Johnson was still alive—he lived where the library is now and his totem pole was not far from there. And he knew the history—he was the one who took my people to Annette Island. He had potlatched with them in the Prince Rupert area in Canada, a long time ago. And when the

89

Conrad Mather

Tsimshians were looking for land near Kasaan, he knew some of their language and said, "Whek, whek," which meant, "Brother, brother, what are you doing?" in Tsimshian. "We're looking for a place." "Oh, I know just the place." So Chief Johnson showed them Annette Island. He said, "My [Tlingit] people camp here in the summer, good running water, flat ground."

So the Tsimshians landed on Annette Island, back when my mother and dad were children. Their leader was Father Duncan and he was a real good missionary from London, England. He built a nice community in Canada known as Old Metlakatla with a church and a marching band. My dad played in the band and my mom sang.

And Father Duncan wanted to learn Tsimshian and there was a Tsimshian boy who wanted to learn English. And they taught each other. So after six months Father Duncan learned the language and gave his first sermon in it. He kept the language going. He used it in the school.

And all the people became Christians. And the reason why they had to leave Canada was because Father Duncan was competing with the Hudson Bay Company on goods—furs and things. So when the big English navy ship came to blow up the Metlakatla village—this is the story we heard, you know—Father Duncan went to the captain, who was Church of England Christian. So the captain told Father Duncan, "You can stay one year, but you better be out when I come back a year from now."

So Father Duncan told the Tsimshian people—they had one year to move to a new village site. This was all because the Hudson Bay said Father Duncan was giving nothing but trouble, reducing the price of furs. So he and the Tsimshians came to Alaska to look for land.

Don't forget they had a cannery in Old Metlakatla. They made money. They had a sawmill. Because of Father Duncan, Indians didn't wear Indian blankets, but dressed like white folks. They ate out of dishes like white folks and had Victorian houses. I mean, he advanced us 50 years.

Then Father Duncan went to Washington, D.C., but couldn't get in to see the president. I don't know which president it was, but of course the president's a big wheel. So he went to the Washington

Episcopal Cathedral. There he talked to the minister and the minister says, "The president's wife is a member of the church and she's in with the altar guild. You come and tell her your story."

So Father Duncan did, and the president's wife told her husband. And the president saw William Duncan. The president said, "Go anywhere in Alaska, but you've got to promise me when you get land and you bring your people there, you can't turn away any other Indians if they want to live with you." That was the agreement. So Father Duncan got a 100-year lease of the land.

As the years went by, the community on Annette grew, and in 1902 their marching band went to Seattle to give a concert. My dad played in it. Sousa marches. For intermission my dad's first cousin sang. She had a beautiful soprano voice. They were all dressed in their Indian outfits.

One of the guys danced like a big chief, and they sang a Tsimshian war song that was absolutely tremendous. And after they were done singing, my aunt sang it while the chief danced. "The Last of the Warriors." So years later when we got into the Indian School with the curio store, my dad put the war song into music where you could play it on the piano. And we sold it to the tourists for 50 cents a copy.

When I was a kid at the Indian School we used to guide tourists and we made good money. We took the tourists to the Chief Johnson pole, up to the Indian School, down to the F.I.P. [Fidalgo Island Packing] cannery and my dad's St. Elizabeth's Church and to a totem park where the junior high is now. We had four totems there— the Thunderbird, the Captain Cook pole, the Lincoln totem and the Wolf totem. That area by the [Schoenbar] junior high was wilderness when I was a kid. We took the tourists to watch salmon jumping up the falls.

Anyway in 1936 here comes a big ship and I guided Robert Taylor, the big movie star of the period. We went to the Indian School, where my dad's totems were on display. He bought my dad's big totems. And he had a "double" with him and he snuck off the boat. So all the girls waiting to see Robert Taylor get off the vessel saw his "double" instead. And when you finished your tour you waited for your tip on the dock. Robert Taylor tipped me $10, which was a big fortune. But I'll never forget a group of teachers who were making $60 a month in the states during those years. After I guided them around, one of them says, "I gave him a quarter and that's enough."

Another guy guided Frank Morgan who played the Wizard of Oz in the movie. And all the kids were running around, "The Wizard of Oz! The Wizard of Oz!"

And I guided around a royal family from England. The woman asked me what I wanted for Christmas and I said a movie projector and it came with the royal seal on the box. And when Elizabeth was crowned Queen of England, I saw her picture on the front page. And I said, "There's the royal, royal . . . oh, my God!" These were the people I had guided around.

The Ketchikan area is where the Tsimshian Indians used to come to gather bark. They call it bark country. And we're the bark people. And we were also the producers of goat hair—you know, goat fur. There were lots of goats in Canada and goats would run through the bushes and the hair would drop off in the spring and this is what the Tsimshians picked like cotton.

The anthropologist who rented my downstairs apartment showed me what the real Indians dressed like before the white men came. Bark coats loaded with goat hair, bare bottoms, moccasins out of deerskin that came way up like boots. They had a bark hat, like a rain hat, like a Chinese. He showed me how they sat to keep warm.

When I was a kid we had a lot of Indian food like boiled fish, smoked salmon, canned deer meat and stuff like that. My mother would put up 400 jars in the summer. All the Indians did. They all went to camps. There was one Tsimshian camp called China Town right across from Mountain Point. My Uncle Casper Mather had a cabin there.

And we all had to pick berries. My mother said, "Don't break the branches, or there won't be any berries tomorrow." So we had to be careful not to break the salmonberry, blueberry, huckleberry branches, you know. Yeah, she put up lots of berries in quart jars.

We also had ooligan grease that came from the Tsimshians in

Canada. That was the time when the natives ate their own food and when I was a kid there were only two Indians that had cancer because the Indian food was healthy.

I went to Wrangell Institute, a boarding school for Indians. But my dad died just at the outbreak of World War II and I had to come home. At the time my mother was the missionary worker for St. Elizabeth's. So I graduated from Ketchikan High School in 1943.

How I got in the Coast Guard is phenomenal. I didn't know that my dad and my uncle Casper had captain's licenses for tugboats, real honest-to-God licenses. They were the only Indians in the whole Territory that had them. So my dad worked on tugboats. You know, in those days you had to tell, "Don't go here, don't go there, there's rocks there."

And there was a young officer on the Coast Guard cutter, Captain Zeusler, and he got to know my dad. He belonged to the same faith—Episcopal. And they were young captains at the same time.

So when I was drafted, they were sending all the draftees over to the big army base at Annette Island. And Father Anderson from St. John's told me, "Instead of going over there, join the Coast Guard down at the base here." So I went down there but they wouldn't swear me in. They said they would send me to the army base at Annette Island. So I told Father Anderson what happened and he called Captain Zeusler who said, "Tell Conrad to come down here now."

When I got down there I was inducted into the Coast Guard. And as the years went by, Zeusler made Admiral. His big office was in Seattle. I went to see him and we went to lunch.

He was the one that sent me to Medical Corpsman School. One week in and I didn't have to go to boot camp. There were only two non-whites in a class of 200 in New York City, one black boy and one Indian—me. Of course we became the best of friends. Then I was stationed at Florence, Oregon, at the lifeboat station. I was the Medical Corpsman. I told the guys there I knew the Admiral. "Oh, sure. Oh, sure." He came by for an inspection. And he asked our commander, "Are you keeping this man busy?" And I was the first one to be discharged from that base when the war ended.

94

After several years I got out of the service and came home. We had a new priest at St. Elizabeth's. So I bought this house for my mother and my brother. Yeah, and then I taught in Sitka for many years. In '62 I came back to Ketchikan and taught at White Cliff School, at the junior high and Valley Park. And then I taught native culture for several years.

The Tsimshian Indians, of course, are the ancient tribe. I'm a member of the Tsimshian Tribal Council. I'm the secretary. We are the ones that gave the Beynon papers to the University. William Beynon was a half-breed Tsimshian who was raised in Vancouver, B.C. He was hired by the anthropologist Boas, who lived among the Tsimshians in Canada for 11 years. Beynon went around to the Indians and they gave him information. At that time they were fishing and hunting to eat. He was able to see a lot of elders who remembered the past, and told about the stories and how the Tsimshians gathered food. So he put all the stories that were told into this big 10,000-page book.

The University is working on it now. We are going to have classes at the University and we are going to read parts that have the Tsimshian writing and record it, 'cause there's only about 20 of us left that speak the language. But it will be like a college class and others can come in and see and hear about the Beynon papers.

It's a huge history with tremendous stories.

Margaret Griffin McCombs

Old fisher ladies do learn some things well.

One of eight children of Patrick and Julia Griffin, Margaret grew up on a homestead two miles north of Kasaan, where the family had settled after arriving in Alaska in 1917. In 1938 she and her husband Reuben bought Knudsen's homestead north of Ketchikan and proved up on an adjacent homesite, where they lived a frontier lifestyle. Her story is one of independence, self-reliance and hard work difficult to imagine today. As Margaret wrote in her 1989 memoir, "None of my heirs will have experiences the same as many I have lived in Alaska."

I was born in Chehalis, Washington, June 18, 1907. We lived in little mill towns when I was young because my dad followed the sawmills. And then when I was 10 years old my family migrated to Alaska where my grandfather Jacob Leibrandt was a prospector and a logger. And the family's been here ever since. I found living in Alaska quite a change from Washington. I'd never seen salt water before, or rowboats that really floated. All those down on the lakes had patches and bailing cans! But we children really enjoyed coming to this country because we had more freedom. I was in the fourth grade when we came up and I graduated from the Kasaan School in the eighth grade in 1922.

My parents filed on 23 acres of land two miles north of Kasaan and that was our home base for several years. We were obliged to clear and use a certain percent of the acreage in order to prove up on the place. This was done between schooling and what have you. A government foot trail connected us to the village and to the It Mine, two miles beyond our place. It was a nice place to grow up because there was freedom and lots of things to do—

Margaret Griffin McCombs

boating and mountain climbing and fishing out front and of course work on the home place kept us busy.

We had hot water—*after* we carried it from the well to the stove and heated it, *and* chopped the wood for the fire. And we had the old-fashioned scrub boards for washing clothes. And the wood was beach wood that we rescued from the saltwater and cut into lengths to fit the fire. There weren't many dull moments! Everyone was busy and had something to do. We enjoyed the big strawberry patch that mother planted. We used to pick them in dishpans. And then we cleared enough acreage for potatoes. There was no market for potatoes so we ate 'em during the winter.

The social life in Kasaan was rather interesting because the town people had socials and whatnot and raised money to have a nice town hall. And the ladies could bake very nicely and they had pie socials and get-togethers and we were all invited. And the dances in the summer time were a lot of fun. Cannery crews came and everybody danced with everybody. You didn't say no to anybody! And we had music of various sorts—it wasn't very professional but it was music and provided entertainment.

I had two older sisters, Gertrude and May, and a younger sister Rose, my brother Sam, then another sister Cynthia, another brother Bill and the baby sister Yvonna. We all helped clear the land, had to cut brush and dig the soil to prepare it for gardens, and the little kids enjoyed climbin' the trees. Every time they had spare time, you'd find them up in the trees. And we loved to beachcomb. We had a beach right in front and we swam there in the summertime.

My brother Sam built himself a boat out of an old tree or slab of timber, I don't know what it was, really. But when he sat on it he was wet. But he boated all around on his "boat." My grandfather had a dory when we first went there, but my older sister was used to a lake where you pulled the boat up ashore and it stayed there. Well, she pulled the boat up and walked off and the boat walked off, too—with the tide!

We never got it back; we didn't have another one to chase it. But it was all a learning process, I guess.

There was a cannery in Kasaan, and the older girls got work immediately in the summer. And after a few years I did, too. Wages were like 10 cents an hour for 11 hours, so I would make $1.10 a day. And my dad gave me a new name—"Dollar-Ten." The last year I worked there I was helping to label the cans and by then I got 45 cents an hour. When I figured it up, I figured I got an extra day's pay and when I went to the China boss and told him about it, he said, "No! My figures are better!" He said he gave me the extra day for working hard, and I wasn't to dispute his wages!

In the wintertime I went to school. The school just went to the eighth grade. One teacher, one big room. There were about 30 kids when I was there. In the eighth grade I was more or less by myself. The teacher assigned my lessons, but I studied by myself. I was doing what you'd call the janitor work around the school. One winter I stayed with the teacher because she was a little leery about living alone there. I had a bedroom in the schoolroom.

Reuben came to work in the cannery and that's when I really met him. He came up here on an old sailboat with his father and a couple of cousins and they didn't get along—there were too many bosses on the boat. So Reuben took off on his own to work in the mines, Russian Brown Mine and Harris Creek Mine, and then he came to work at the cannery. I was 15 then. He's the only one I ever went out with. He took me to the community dances and whatnot at Kasaan. And then I went to school in Ketchikan for a year at Kayhi and he came in whenever he could get from Kasaan to Ketchikan, which wasn't very often.

The next year we got married, on Alaska Day, October 18, 1923. I was 16. My older sister was already married so she had a cold lunch for us—turkey, if I remember right. Then my dad got someone to bake a big wedding cake. And ice cream. Then my sister May was working at the old Dream Theater and the show "Rip Van Winkle" was on, so [theater owner] Mrs. Hoover invited us to come and see it.

Reuben worked at the cannery in Kasaan—running the fish house, helping rebuild a cannery tender, and then operating cannery tenders. We bought the old Baronovich home in Kasaan for $400 and added a woodshed and chicken house. Wages weren't high but we saved enough to buy our *Trego* in 1928 for $1500.

After that we lived on the boat, a 36-foot troller, a double ender, and traveled all over Southeast Alaska. That first summer we watched a trap at Lemesurier Point for the Quadra Cannery for $900. That gave us independence; and afterward fishing and trapping kept us self-supporting on a modest scale.

In the wintertime, we moored at whichever harbor we were going to trap. The snow was deeper then. We trapped mink, mostly, and land otters, in all kinds of weather. Our trap lines followed the beach. My brothers went with us some years. I tended the rowboats for them when they were setting the traps and I'd ferry 'em from one place to the next, you know. I'd put one ashore with some traps and go ahead in and put off another one and then come back and pick the other one up. The first year I rowed, but after that we always had a motor on the rowboat.

Our headquarters was here in Ketchikan. Ketchikan, well, it had its limits back then. Herring Cove was at one end of the road and the old garbage dump at the other. I knew everybody by sight and knew where they belonged, even if I didn't know them personally. Everybody was well-known then—couldn't get away with anything. Now you can walk into some place and they don't even know you. Reuben and I went to shows; we loved to go to shows. We'd go to the ice cream parlors. Kubley's daughters had an ice cream parlor downtown.

We'd come to town for the Fourth of July and it was a lot of fun in those days! They did more things, more water sports, not so much parade. The seine boats would have tug-o-wars. They had boxing matches with blindfolded people on an open scow, and log rolling and rowboat races. The Coast Guard people were out there one time, rowing, and I nearly laughed myself sick! The two boats came together and they were slappin' each other with the oars!

In 1938 Reuben and I bought Captain Knudson's homestead and filed on the adjoining homesite as well. We built a house and boatshed and I had a nice garden spot there. I had goats and chickens and kids. We had milk goats, shipped them in from Oregon, because Yvonna couldn't tolerate canned milk. Yvonna was born in 1943 and Marion in 1945. I had to learn to milk the critters. Reuben was sick one day and I thought, "Well, I'll milk her." But Daisy, she didn't like it and turned her head and told me, "Bleahhhh!" She'd had enough. I finally learned how to do it.

We dammed up a little creek for water. And when it dried up in the summertime we went over to Clover Pass creek and got water. My girls attended the little school on Potter Road. My husband helped build that school. It was in the early 1940s. He stayed home from fishing long enough to get the school ready. The girls went there until Yvonna was in sixth grade and then they were missing too much, after-school events and things, so we moved in to town. We'd had a bad fishing season and didn't have much to go on, so I started work at the Tongass Laundry. I was doing housecleaning on the side and later did custodial work for the schools. We stayed with friends and family and then started renting.

My husband tried custodial work in the schools but he couldn't do it. He was getting sick. One night I saw him standing there and he was hardly able to breathe. He was trying to swing those big mops. I said, "You quit. You don't have to do this." Then we went to Tongass Towers. I didn't need to live there but Reuben did. He needed the elevator and the heat. My husband died in 1966.

I bought a trailer, and I needed a full-time job. They had a crash course, training people in shorthand, bookkeeping and typing. I wasn't any good at typing so I concentrated on bookkeeping and I got on with Heckman's [Department Store] in the office. I was there almost seven years.

I've carried on with various jobs since I've been alone. For about a year I cooked on the *Heidi H.* Twice on board that boat I was asked to hold a course while the skipper worked on deck. When he returned, he was surprised I hadn't deviated from the course. Old fisher ladies do learn some things well.

Being 13 years older than me, Reuben taught me to be independent, which is a wonderful gift. Reuben worked hard and I worked as a partner under his guidance. I always conceded he was the boss, but treated him like my best friend. It seemed to work for us.

I think of those first years when he and I were free to roam. I enjoyed my children and am glad I had 'em and everything, but I

101

look back on those years when my husband and I were together, roaming around and, well, I enjoyed the freedom. We had a few ups and downs, but nothing bad. And fishing is always tough, and trapping tougher yet, if you work at it the way we did. But those years we spent at sea are treasured memories; those were the best times of my life.

Del Richardson

The last thing in the world I ever wanted was a steady job.

Del came to Ketchikan March 19, 1945. During World War II, he served in the Merchant Marines and was on a tanker at Normandy in June of '44. The law was that when the ship reached the first American port a merchant marine could "pay off." So Del debarked at Galveston, Texas, and traveled to Seattle, planning to sail the Asiatic theater of war. To that end he bought a steerage ticket on the SS Alaska *and came to Ketchikan. Shortly thereafter the war ended and he decided to make Alaska his home.*

I came to Ketchikan to sail coastwise to the Aleutians. I sailed on the Northland Transportation. I made one trip and then I came back. I shoulda signed on in Seattle for wherever I was gonna go in Asia, but I didn't. I wanted to come up here. I figured it would be the best way to see Alaska, you know. We pretty well knew the war was goin' to be over. And all of sudden they dropped the A-bomb, and that ended the war.

I liked it here. There was only 3,000 to 3,500 people, that's all there was—on Prince of Wales and everything. The highway was just a dirt road, two narrow lanes. I just wanted to be where there weren't a lot of people. Now we got too many.

My first job here was at the spruce mill. In those days, they cut 24 hours a day at the mill because the Army was takin' it all. They didn't care what they bought, rough, knots . . . So I took a job scaling in the well deck. You measure every log, and that tells the head sawyer how much he's cut during the day. The well deck is where they pull the logs up. But the noise was terrible; it would

Del Richardson

just drive ya nuts. It was a steam catapult that kicked them logs. I got tired of them. I got 60 cents an hour; that was the goin' wage.

Then Beaver Falls power plant came about. I knew Einar Erickson, whose father was superintendent of the Territorial Road Commission here. Einar wanted to know if I'd ever surveyed, and I said, "Well, no." He said, "That's all right, do you want to go to work?" He said, "You can just help me and you can have 90 cents an hour." So I thought that was pretty good and I went, and that was a good job. There weren't a lot of men, there may have been 30 total. We punched that tunnel from Upper Silvis down to the dam and the power plant.

But the last thing in the world I ever wanted was a steady job. I couldn't stand that 'cause I wanted to go do what I wanted to do, like trappin' in the winter. I wouldn't think of takin' a steady job.

I trapped mostly marten and mink in Boca de Quadra, some otter. Prices were good in those days. We got $31 for a mink; we got $100 and over for marten. Today if you get $7 for marten, you're lucky. And $100 in those days was more than $1000 today. Gas was nine cents, diesel was six, seven cents. We made a lot of money. I had a friend, Charley Rice, he was 30 years older than me and had a lot of experience, and I trapped with him. During the war, see, they quit trappin' 'cause of the war effort. They didn't need mink skins, or otter. So there had been no trappin' since 1940. And the buildup of fur was tremendous. I got in just at the right time. It was a good three years. Then they decided they were payin' too much, and the price started slippin', and it never did come back.

Also in territorial days I worked in the predator control for around five years. We worked from, say, November 15 to April first. We'd quit before the bear come out in the spring; we didn't want to kill anything but wolves. We'd kill, oh, 100-120 wolves a year. I did that for five years, and then we had these people come in and they were against poison and they stopped us. And the wolf population got so big they were eatin' all the deer.

I went logging before the power saw came in. We had a hand saw, a "Swedish fiddle," you know. And there'd be a team of us. There'd be a bucker and two fallers, and I was one of the fallers, and the young guy with me was the bucker. And we'd go out and we'd fall timber, by the thousand, they called it "bushlin'." We'd do that for a couple, three, four months. We were workin' what we called "gyppo camps." There was 12 men to a camp, one set of fallers, and a guy drivin' a Cat and there'd be another guy doin' somethin' else. Real small camps. One cook. They would scale the timber—that would be measurin' it—and then you got so much a thousand board feet. We'd work six hours a day and make $30 to $40 . . . the ordinary person was makin' about $10 a day.

The power saw came in about five or six years after we started. I thought it was goin' to be nice, but the first power saw was electric. You had to drag around a generator and the generators were as big as a kitchen. 'Course the Cat did that. And it took two men to run this danged electric saw. It was really harder than pullin' the hand saw. Well, then the McCullough power saw came in. It was a dandy saw. One man could run it. So that was fine except it made so much noise. It would drive ya nuts to hear that all day long. And the smoke comin' out of the saw—I just quit bushlin'. Too much work!

I did a lot of seagoing rafts. In them days it was just like it is today. The Forest Service wouldn't let you sell any logs unless they were canted. In other words the sides had to be cut, or some labor done on 'em here in Alaska. Well, they had a strike, both this mill and the Juneau mill. They piled up millions of feet of logs. Well, the teredos were eatin' 'em, those bugs—wormwood is what they call it. They'll eat a log 'til there's nothin' left and it'll just sink. So the Forest Service gave permission to put out sea-goin' rafts and export 'em to Asia, and most of 'em went to Seattle. They were big rafts— 700-800-feet long. I worked on a couple, and finally they gave me the contract to build 'em because I hadn't lost any logs. So I exported out of Sitka, and out of Fitzgibbon Cove. It was pretty good money. Hard work. But there again we could shut down in the winter when it got icy.

In those days there weren't no truck loggin', it was all long logs; and the logs would be 80- to 100-feet, which is what the timber companies wanted. So they BSed the Forest Service. They said they needed what they called "skin-tighteners"—after you rolled short hemlock logs, you put these long spruce logs around 'em. Belling-ham Pulp & Timber shipped out millions of feet of this beautiful spruce. And they called 'em "test rafts." Of course, it was nothing but a gimmick by Puget Sound Pulp & Timber and Bellingham Pulp & Timber to get all the spruce out of here they could.

I had Bob Bishop as a partner and we were out at Ward Cove, before the mill even got started. We built tremendous rafts. The last one was 2.4 million [board feet]; that's a lot of logs. I think she was 680 feet long and 48 feet wide in the stern, and 29 feet in the bow. We tried to make 'em like a boat so they towed better. Anyway, we shipped millions of feet of beautiful spruce out. They just cut 'em for lumber, ya know, they'd never seen logs like that. Made beautiful lumber. Those companies were rubbin' their hands. And of course they made pulp out of the hemlock. Those test rafts—it was just a gimmick. They got away with it. In them days you only had a few Forest Ser-vice people. You didn't have all these do-gooders. I was here when they had only four Forest Service people. Now under every bush you got a Forest Service guy lookin' at you.

When I quit logging, I went into the hunting and guiding busi-ness. I went first with Campbell Church—that was a big outfit out of Seattle. I was a guide, hunted bear. We had mostly European hunters, some from Texas, New York. I was on the *Westward*, and the *Onawa*, the *Acania*, the *Deer Leap*. I was on all those big boats, 80-footers. It was a good job.

After Campbell Church, I went on my own. I had L.J. Skaggs of the Payless Drug Company [as a client]. I'd have him 30 days a year. I'd put in maybe 90 days a year in the hunting and fishing busi-ness. And I had a couple of my own boats. Bob Bishop would guide for me. He knew a lot of people and we'd get clients that way. I made a lot of guided trips. We'd take, say, a two-week trip. We'd take four or five a year, two in the spring, maybe three in the fall. But we were here in the best of the times. Bruce Johnstone, Handlogger Jackson, and me, Bob Bishop, Jens Jensen. At one time Jens and I and Eldon Coon were the only charter boat guys in the whole country. And now look at 'em, God Almighty! 'Course they don't have boats as big as we had, but they're making more money than we did. When we went out, if we had to work 20 hours a day, we worked 20 hours a day. But these guys go four or eight hours and they're tied back up again. We never knew such a thing as that. The Mellons out of Pittsburg, the Mellon Steel Company, we'd take them out for 35 days!

One time Bob Bishop and I got this trip with this guy from South Africa, a very rich man who sold gold-mining equipment. He had only one leg, and he traveled all through Europe. These rich guys that came over here didn't bring their wives normally; they brought what they called "traveling companions."

Well, this guy's traveling companion was Georgette and she was a Belgian gal. She was about 30 or 35 and he was about 70, quite a difference in age. Anyway, Bob and I chartered the *Princeton Hall*— which was owned by Roy Hedman, the US Marshal here—and took her up to Juneau to meet this guy and Georgette. We pick them up and get down to the boat and this guy says, "We gotta get some rain gear for Georgette." He handed me a big wad of money and said, "Take her and get her whatever she wants." So, fine with me. Bob stays aboard with this guy. Anyway we get the rain gear and a rifle and we got her a bunch of stuff, and we come back to the boat. So we pulled out of Juneau and we went to Warm Springs Bay and Baranof and all over the country.

In the meantime, the FBI was lookin' for this Georgette. They had a FBI agent posted at the damn Juneau airport, but he missed her for some reason or other. And I didn't know nothing about this 'til I got back. Anyway we got the trip and she got a giant bear and the one-legged guy, he got a bear with Bob Bishop. All during this trip, just her and me were hunting. We'd go out seal hunting in the morning and we'd go bear hunting in the afternoon. It was daylight 'til 11:00 and then we'd have dinner. All during the day she'd ask me, did I know anything about Ladd Air Field, or Eielson Air Base, and what about the Coast Guard Base in Ketchikan? And what about Annette Island? I couldn't figure out why she was so interested. So I just let it go. I didn't tell her anything that wasn't common knowledge. I didn't know anything about Eielson or Ladd; the Coast Guard I knew about, but, Christ, a BB gun down there would be a big weapon!

Anyway, I get back home. Barbara, my wife, says, "What have you been doing?" I said, "What are you talking about? What have you been doing? I've been working!" "Well," she says, "the police and the FBI are lookin' for you!" I thought, "She's jokin'."

But she wasn't.

The FBI come here. So I says, "Well, I didn't do anything." And they said, "Well, you've gotta go down to the police station." So I had to go down to the police station and meet the FBI. It turns out that Georgette's a Russian spy. The FBI guy says, "What ports did you hit? I want your log book." I says, "We left the boat in Juneau. You gotta go to Juneau to get the log book."

Anyway, I kept saying, "I didn't do anything!" And he said, "I know *you* didn't, but *she* did." And he says, "We were told to pick her up and arrest her at the Juneau Airport, but we missed her." And they were lookin' all over for her. Finally they found out that the US Marshal owned the damned boat that she was on; that made it worse yet!

They went around to every post office—all them little ports had a post office in them days—to see what letters she had mailed. They did all that. Probably a good summer vacation for the FBI. That's what it amounted to. But for them to be gumshoeing all over Alaska, she had to be pretty high up. She's a buxom-lookin' woman; not a thin woman. Blue eyes and blonde hair. She could have probably brought men out, you know, one of them kind of women. 'Course that's what they had her for.

The FBI knew where she left from, when she left and when she got here. Except the stupe of a FBI agent missed her. Christ! The Juneau Airport wasn't very big in them days. They should have been able to catch her, a blonde and an old man with one leg?

So anyway, the FBI guy says, "If you hear from her, well, we want to know about it." I said, "Oh, yeah, you bet."

Well, what she wanted from me was 10 otter skins. I was trappin' otter in the winter. And we'd get up to 70, 80, 100 otter sometimes. And I told her I'd sell 'em to her. It was legitimate, but I didn't particularly want anybody to know about it. So I get this letter out of Cuba about three months later: "Where's my otter skins?" And she reminisced all about the trip.

And I read the letter and of course I didn't want Barbara seein' it, so I tore the damn letter all up and threw it away. So one afternoon I was standin' on the corner down by Tongass, talkin' to somebody, and this gol-danged guy come and I could tell he was a damn dick of some kind. And he tapped me on the shoulder and you know how they put their FBI thing out. And I said, "What the hell did I do now?"

Well, it was what I didn't do. They had intercepted the letter here at the Post Office. He says, "You got a letter from Georgette." And I said, "Yeah, I guess I did." He said, "I thought you told me you were goin' to give it to me." And I said, "Well, yeah, but I didn't want to." He said, "Well, I don't know, there was nothin' in it anyway." I said, "Yeah, I know; all it had to do with was these otter skins. I didn't do nothin'."

Apparently, they had to assume I was linked in this spy ring. This letter came out of Cuba. And 'course she was down there as a Russian espionage agent. And I wondered why she could shoot so good. Christ! Most men couldn't hit a bear, but she could hit seal heads at 100-150 yards and she could use a knife like you couldn't believe. You couldn't believe that woman!

But that's what she was. They finally captured her. I don't know what they did with her, but she was an intelligence agent for the KGB and here I hunted with her for 30 days! It was a 30-day trip! And I had no idea. Bob about had a heart attack. He thought he was goin' to jail and so was everybody else.

The guiding went on for quite a few years, and then the danged pulp mill came in. Every bay you went into, on whatever island—Admiralty, Baranof or Chicagof—there was a big load of loggers that would disrupt your hunting. Bear get scared, you can't have a big lot of noise. And it got embarrassing, these trips cost a lot of money. And you had to get Europeans or Texans or Californians or New Yorkers who could afford these trips. So I just quit the hunting. The only hunting I would ever do would be just me and one other guy. That would be in the fall for bear and it would have to be some-one I knew.

The hunting like we had is all gone; never will be again. First of all, there aren't any guides who know anything; they come up here and get a license and half of them don't know what they're doin'. And there's not the interest there used to be, either. Oh, people like to hunt, but a lot of them can't pay the price it takes to go do it anymore. And the bear are not as thick; it's pretty tough to get those big bears; they're pretty tough to come by. What you've got now is fishing; people can afford a day or two of fishing, but you can't do a day or two of bear hunting. Some of these bear hunts cost $40,000 to $50,000. So it's all changed.

And the country's changed. In the early days of hunting, we'd see maybe one bear-hunting boat in the whole trip, in the whole two weeks to 30 days. Toward the end we were seeing a lot. And nowadays there might be 15 people in hunting with ya. And that's embarrassing, you know, to charge them people that kind of money for that.

But over the years I met a lot of interesting people and had some good jobs. I didn't do anything I didn't want to do. I ain't gonna either!

Maxine Robertson

The fog rolled in and I thought of "Brigadoon."
It was just like that.

Before Maxine Robertson was born in Washington State, her father had been in Alaska, working on gold dredges. He went first to Nome, then to Dawson City. He brought home some prized possessions—a beautiful walrus tusk cribbage board, some gold he had panned on the sands of Nome and stored in a little glass vial, and a deck of cards adorned with pictures of the White Pass and Yukon Railroad. And he would tell his children stories about the wonderful life he'd led in the far north. Maxine grew up fascinated by the stories and Alaskan mementos.

All the stories and things my father talked about made me want to come to Alaska. But when the time came, my mother said, "We can't let Maxine go up there alone. She may never come back. We can't tell what will happen to her."

My father replied, "I had an interesting life up there. I wouldn't want to tell her, no, that she can't go."

So that was my open sesame. I said, "I'm going."

A teacher who taught at a school called Charcoal Point in Ketchikan had contacted me and told me of an opening. She told me where to be interviewed. That was the beginning, in 1932.

I got the job at Charcoal Point and taught second grade there for a year, for $50 a month. Then the school closed, and they could not afford to keep the additional teachers. So there were no jobs for the five teachers from Charcoal Point School. So I went back home to my parents for the summer. But the Commissioner of Education Tony Karnes—who had been an instructor in Ketchikan before he

Maxine Robertson

was elected to the job—told me not to worry, that he'd find a place for all the Charcoal Point teachers.

But when I had not heard from him by August, I commenced to get worried and thought I'd better look for a school down there. So I did. And the day one of the school board members came to my house to tell me I had a job, I received a telegram from Tony Karnes, saying he had a place for me at Hope, Alaska. So I knew that's where I was going to go, because I had friends in Ketchikan I could stop to see on the way.

I was excited. I went to the Alaska Steamship Company and asked them how to get to Hope. They said, "We can get you to Seward, but we don't know how you get to Hope." Well, it turned out to be not such a problem. When I came and stayed in Ketchikan for a week before going north, a friend introduced me to the Schallerers who were opening a photography shop here. They had lived up there, and they had a niece who was living in Hope. So I got good information before I started out.

Hope was a little mining town that hadn't had a school for 11 years. They had this old school building. You had to go past Sunrise, another little mining town, to get there. I went in with the boy who delivered the mail. He had a little Ford that he could put skids on the back so he could run in the winter before the snow got too deep. Then he'd run a dog team. So people in Hope would get their mail about every four weeks. This was 1933, '34.

At Christmas time everyone in Hope, all the miners and everybody, filled the hall. And we all took food and gifts for the children. We only had candlelight; we didn't have electricity. But we had a nice get-together.

I'm glad I experienced those things. I'd go with others up into the hills to bring down a quarter of a moose to thaw. I'd go with my skis on and we'd bring the meat from where it hung in the trees, where it was cached, and everyone would have moose meat.

When I left Hope, I planned to go across Turnagain Arm and down the railroad. But we had a storm, so I couldn't do that. And the man who was in charge of the road came from Moose Pass and I rode on the Caterpillar all the way with him; that is, till we joined where you could get a car and go the rest of the way. That was an experience! He'd run up against this snowfield and back down, then try it again. But we got out that way.

I taught in Hope one year and came back to Ketchikan. I was engaged to be married to a young man here, Harry Peterson. We had kept it a secret because Harry was a volunteer fireman and Ketchikan Fire Department had a habit of playing terrible nuptial tricks on their members. We were wed in a clandestine ceremony July 2, 1934, and afterward we went to our little home on Deermount Street that Harry had bought and painted. It was nice and cozy. We settled in for normal living, but it would only last for a very brief period.

I was involved with the Girl Scouts and went to summer camp with them at Herring Cove for a few days. Just a day or two after I returned, Harry said he wasn't feeling well. I took care of him a few days at home, but when he didn't get better, I called Doctor Ellis. He said to get Harry to the hospital right away.

There were three people in the hospital with pneumonia. They did everything for Harry. But he needed oxygen, and there was a big military ship down at Dixon Entrance escorting a group of fliers. They could make oxygen on the ship but their men couldn't take off and deliver it. So Art Liljestrand and Bob Ellis volunteered and flew down and brought back oxygen. But it was too late—it didn't save Harry's life. By the 22nd of August he was gone. That was a sad time. He was a robust, healthy young man and he died of pneumonia during a beautiful hot summer.

After Harry died, I knew I would return to teaching. A friend sent a telegram to Tony Karnes, telling of my situation. He wired back, "Offer you the school at Hyder. You can go one week late and make it up at the end of the year." And he sent his condolences.

So I had to start making plans. I had to rent our little house. I packed my things and was going to go to Hyder on the mailboat. But Bob Ellis was flying a charter and offered me a ride. Well, I had never flown on a plane. He was going to land near Stewart but it was pretty foggy so we landed on the canal and bounced around and some of us, including me, got a little seasick.

Anyway, people met us at the dock. The ladies had heard I was coming and they were just more than kind. They found me a little parsonage to rent and some loaned me this and some loaned me that 'til I had a nice little cottage fitted out and was ready to get back to work.

People came to get acquainted. One woman took me under her wing and said, "The first nice weekend we'll go see the Premier Mine [outside of Stewart, B.C.]. The gardens there are beautiful." So we did.

I just joined in with whatever the people were doing. They were having whist parties at the Pioneer Hall in Hyder. One time I made sandwiches and I was wearing a long dress and serving these sandwiches when I met a young man with a strange accent. Finally I got up the nerve to ask him, "What nationality are you anyway?"

Well, of course, he was from Scotland. This was Al and he was the landscaper at the Premier Mine, responsible for the beautiful gardens. He would look at me with those piercing eyes and I avoided him all I could because I didn't want to get mixed up with anybody. I just didn't want to go through that again.

He was kind and understanding, but I wasn't ready to be serious. He'd write letters to me in Hyder but I wouldn't answer them. Finally he wrote and said that if I didn't answer his letter he was coming to see me. I didn't, and he did. We became friends.

And the flowers! He was always sending me flowers while I was in Hyder, when I went south to summer school, and after I moved back to Ketchikan the following year. I couldn't forget about him. He wouldn't let me forget about him!

In 1935 I was teaching fourth grade at White Cliff School. In late fall Al came over for a visit. He enjoyed Ketchikan but after a few days he returned to the Premier Mine, continuing to write and send flowers. Finally he convinced me to return to Hyder for New Year's Eve and attend the Premier Mine Cabaret, which was a festive community occasion.

That was the beginning of my new life. As soon as I arrived, Al had a diamond ring ready for me. I accepted it. We became engaged, and were married the following summer [1936] in a little chapel at the College of Puget Sound, where I'd gone to college.

Al had made arrangements to rent a little house in Stewart. This meant that we would see each other only on weekends because Al had to live and work at the mine during the week. He would come home on weekends even if he had to walk the 15 miles from the mine. After a few months we were able to move into an apartment at the mine and await the arrival of our first child. Ian was born in the little apartment on March 25, 1939.

We knew that the future of the mine was uncertain. What Al really wanted to do was open a florist shop in Ketchikan. So in the summer of 1940, we moved to Ketchikan and opened the shop across the street from the Episcopal Church. Al was the only one in town who could do professional floral designing.

Then Pearl Harbor happened and everything changed. All our cool-room space went for the war effort. We closed down, thinking it would be just temporary. We never did reopen. Al spent the war years working for Standard Oil and then he got the job at First National Bank working with Mr. Murkowski.

We bought our house at Mountain Point in 1941 from Dr. Carlson, the optometrist. It had such nice land with it and that's what we wanted so we could raise flowers and vegetables. Tongass Trading Company and Wingren's [Grocery Store] said they'd buy whatever we could grow.

We lived in that house for 34 years. We added on to the place when it was time for Ian to have his own room, and again when we were going to have Heather.

We enjoyed Mountain Point and were involved in many projects like the construction of the Community Club. We had a little church where I taught Sunday school and a small library where our kids could check out books. Then the ladies organized the Mountain Point Homemakers Club

Our daughter Heather was born in 1947 when Ian was eight years old and well into elementary school. Mountain Point was a good place for children, the out-of-doors. Al built a little boat and we did our share of boating in that till he built another boat with a little top for it. Then finally we got a 16-foot Glass Ply. And we just enjoyed the country.

Al stayed at the bank. He was elected to the Ketchikan School Board and later appointed to the State Board of Education and eventually to the University Board of Regents by Governor Hickel. He was also active in the Lions Club and things.

The time came that I wanted a wintertime job. Because Al was on the school board, I couldn't apply for a teaching job. So I started as a receptionist and mail clerk at the Employment Office and I never got out of there. I became a claims adjuster and then they asked me to manage the office. Our motto was "Jobs for People and People for Jobs" and I enjoyed that—matching up people and jobs.

Al and I were involved from the beginning with the [Ketchikan] Community College. I helped organize an advisory board and served as chairperson and secretary. I was proud to be part of the ceremony when we turned the first shovel full of dirt for our new college.

Al passed away on November 30, 1975, of cancer. I went back to work at the Employment Office and devoted much time to my new granddaughter, Alana.

I thought about how Al and I had planned to get a trailer or motor home and travel. I thought, "I still want to do these things." So I talked to Ian and ended up with a new, fully equipped motor home. Since 1980 I have made four trips to northern Alaska and the Yukon.

Heather, Alana and I have made two trips to Scotland to visit Al's relatives. And the three of us made a very special trip back to Hyder and the Premier Mine, or where the mine used to be. The buildings are gone, but Alana found some enamelware souvenirs that she was sure belonged to Grandpa Al, and some roses he had planted.

When we were coming down the mountain, down from the mine, the fog rolled in and I thought of "Brigadoon," the movie. It was just like that. The Premier Mine, the once-thriving little community, had disappeared, been swallowed up in the mist just like Brigadoon. Still for "just a few bright hours," I was living again the happy times . . . the old friendships . . . the memories.

If Al were still living, we'd be in Ketchikan yet and I wouldn't be moving south. But I'll tell people down south that we had a wonderful life in Alaska. And I remember asking my father about his time in the north, when he was working on the gold dredge at Nome, and he said, "I enjoyed my time up there. I had a wonderful life up there."

Bob Roppel

The pulp mill was all just one big story...

Bob Roppel first came to Alaska in 1929. He returned several times, mostly on jobs for various canneries around the Territory. He did not settle in Ketchikan until 1953, when he went to work for the Ketchikan Pulp Company. At that time the pulp mill was in the early stages of construction and Roppel stayed with the company for more than 20 years, witnessing many changes.

It was pretty bad that first year. I didn't think that mill was gonna make it. We dumped more pulp than we dried. Boy, you'd never get away with that now. See, this mill was the first one—though Weyerhaeuser had a small operation goin' at Longview, Washington—to burn the sulfite liquor. They burnt the liquor from sulfate mills, called craft mills. But this is the first one to burn the magnesium oxide. See, the rest of them all use lime rock. And you couldn't burn lime rock because it would get in there and turn to cement. It took the first two years before we really got it continuously on grade.

Before coming here, I worked in a pulp mill in Oregon City for a few years. Then I quit that and went back to the cannery business. I worked in canneries in the '20s. I went up to Ivanof Bay—about half way between Chignik and Sand Point on the Alaska Peninsula—for Harold Parks. That was in 1952.

We built the cannery there from the beach up. I took a crew with me and we stayed in what they called a *barabara*—it's a hole dug in the ground and it's all boarded up inside and it's got dirt all the way around it. There were 15 of us that stayed in there. The river came right through the cannery and it was good water. That's the reason they put the cannery in there—on account of the water.

Bob Roppel

That first year at Ivanof Bay we weren't supposed to can any fish, but we canned 67,000 cases. We got the fish out of Libby boats. They let 'em sell to us. We set up a one-and-a-half line cannery and we had 50 Filipinos working. Some people from Sand Point came over and helped us build barracks for the workers. It was a gill net and seining operation and we had the *Victory Maid*, the *Dorothea* and the *Robert Eugene*. Then the second year, '53, we put up pretty close to 100,000 cases.

I left there in '53 and the cannery ran for two years after that, then it was sold to Alaska Packers and they closed it down. It later caught fire and burned up.

I met Dave Murdey at Sand Point and we left Ivanof Bay together. It was late September. Bob Richmond, who I knew, told me they were building a pulp mill at Ketchikan, why don't you stop and see it? So Dave Murdey and I stopped here and we both got hired at the pulp mill. It was October of '53. We were two of the first hired.

In a pulp mill you have five crafts. You have millwrights, electricians, machinists, pipe fitters and welders. The millwrights take care of the nuts and bolts, install and overhaul the heavy machinery. I had the auto shop, too. That was a headache. I started out as a millwright, got up to lead millwright, then I ended up as master mechanic.

One of my first jobs as master mechanic was puttin' a new boom in the Whirley. That's that big machine on the dock that goes around and lifts heavy things, like a crane. Washington Whirley. It had air clutches on it and a guy was runnin' it and he was boomin' the thing, goin' to lift the chipper disk. And the air hose broke on the thing and it happened so quick he didn't hit the foot brakes to stop it. The boom dropped and smashed two boxcars. Nobody got hurt, but that was a big job—puttin' in that new boom.

There were eight people killed building that mill. The last fellow was a construction worker, and the mill had started and he was over in the wood room. And he threw the chunk of wood down and the guy runnin' the head rig never turned the power off. And the carriage run over him. There was two killed inside the silo. They were takin' the staging out, unscrewed the nuts. Then there was another one killed outside—they was makin' the tar up for under the

121

tank, and he didn't take the cap off and it blew up. When I left, that tar was still on the silo up there. Then that guy who got killed in the air dryer, Ray was his name. Six on construction and one on the pulp mill. Oh, and the girl—she got caught between two rolls. That makes eight.

It was a dangerous place to work. I run probably the longest of any department without a loss-time accident. I was very strict with [my workers], wouldn't let 'em monkey around, no horseplay. See, we were responsible for them till they got outa the gate, then they were on their own.

The other departments had a lot of turnover, but I never had much with the millwrights. By golly, you could never hire another crew like that—Barney Powell, old man Brack, a bunch of 'em, 30 of 'em. Ernie Smeltzer was a totem carver and iron chink guy for Brindle, we hired him and put him in the finishing room and he did a good job.

You know, there wasn't just one or two stories about the mill; it was all just one big story.

I first come up in '29 on a boat, the *Libby Maine*, as a helper in the engine room. I was 19. We went to all the Libby, McNeil & Libby canneries—George Inlet, over to Craig, Petersburg, Taku and Yakutat—haulin' coal from Seattle. The *Libby Maine* was about the size of one of the Alaska Steam boats—about a 400-foot boat, carried a couple thousand tons. We'd leave from the coal dock in Seattle, which was close to where Sears Roebuck is now. At that time I had no idea I'd be back.

But in '32 I come up again, not to Ketchikan but to Bristol Bay for Libby, McNeil. Them days, our tin cans used to come in flat plates about the size of a small table, and they had to cut 'em up and get about 36 cans out of a sheet. And my job before the season started was taking care of the long seam in the cans, soldering that with a soldering machine. I had three of 'em to run. I had to mix the tin and the lead and keep it at the right temperature. If it got too cold, it got too much on and didn't do a good job, and if you got it too hot, you wouldn't get enough on. I was in the machinist gang. I started out as grease monkey greasin' the machinery and helpin' the machinist with the repair work. Then I got to be iron chink guy, sharpening knives of the iron chink and cleanin' them.

Then we'd come down and bring the fish to the Ames Terminal on Harbor Island. Then we all went up to the Dexter Horton Bank Building and got our money in $20 gold pieces. All cash. God, in those days you could go to a bootleggin' joint, you know, and five cents for a quart of home brew. There was lots of them places up around Seattle. But you didn't dare go in with a $20 gold piece. You went in with quarters and dimes, or you'd get knocked in the head.

I come up again during World War II to get people to come down to Astoria for the tuna run for the Army. The Army was the head of the meat and poultry and fish out of Vancouver, Washington, and they wanted more tuna fishermen. The only place you could get 'em was trollers from Alaska. We come to Ketchikan, Wrangell, Petersburg, Juneau, Sitka and then down to Port Alexander and that's where we got the most of the trollers. We got a lot of 'em to come down, but they didn't fish for us. See, they had a set price on the tuna and those other guys were payin' under the counter, and the guy I was workin' for was afraid because he got investigated when he was sellin' oil to this potato chip outfit. He was afraid to pay these guys under the counter because he'd just squeaked out of that thing.

Then in '47—remember when the guy got blew up in the FIP cannery [in Ketchikan]? They sent me up from Astoria to take his place. So I stayed up here that summer and worked. They'd taken all the line shafts out of the camloft and were puttin' individual motors on. Everything was operated off the line at that time, a line shaft with pulley belts comin' down. And we took 'em off and put the motors on each piece of equipment.

[My wife] Beulah come up in '54 after I got hired at the mill. I met Beulah in Astoria and we got married in '36. Frank is our oldest. And we had Rosanne and Donnie. Otto's the youngest. He was a year old when we moved up. We brought a car, a boat, a big outboard engine, a lawn mower, tools, lathes and grinders, too much stuff. We were really greenhorns on that deal.

Before we got the house we stayed in an apartment on the

eighth floor of the Austin Towers. Eight stories down, and Otto jumping on the bed, right by that flimsy window. Four kids in a two-bedroom apartment!

We've been in this house since 1954. It sits on elevation 14—below high tide. The 14-foot brass marker is right out the window there. When we bought the house, come to find out all we owned was half of the house—from the living room out into the middle of the street. We were greenhorns on that deal, too. The rest of the house was on federal tideland. We didn't get title to it till we become a state. We paid $325 from the living room out for about 400 feet. Later they filled in under the house so it don't move much any more. She used to move pretty good when there was a big log or oil drum under there.

Our yard went halfway out there in the pavement [Tongass Avenue]. It was practically a one-way gravel road back then. A car went by about every half-hour. This whole block was solid with houses. Now our house is the only residence on this side between Third Avenue and the city limits. We paid $10,000 for it. Was offered $200,000 for the place and Beulah—she's the boss around here—turned 'em [Veterans of Foreign Wars] down. Even if they raised the ante it wouldn't do no good. Even old Paul Wingren tried to proposition Beulah, offered us money and an apartment up in that deal down by the bowling alley [Sea Level Condominiums] if we'd sell. But we couldn't have no dog there so that was the end of that.

When I left the mill in July of '75, I had 108 men working for me. I went back to the cannery business—I run the cannery at Wrangell for five years. And in the wintertime I worked on the [state ferry] *Chilkat* for 10 years. I run the engines on the *Chilkat*, and that was a better job than master mechanic at the pulp mill.

William Stensland

Clams on the beach and deer in the woods.

William Stensland's grandparents emigrated from Norway in the early 1860s. His parents, A. Henry and Almena, moved to Alaska in 1912. They purchased 360 acres on Gravina Island where they raised their six sons and three daughters.

Well, I was born in Ketchikan, November 16, 1924. I'm the seventh one of nine—Walter, Tildon, Henry, Minnie, Eva, Lloyd and myself, then the twins Beatrice and George. We lived on Gravina Island. There was only three or four families over there. My father had a dairy on the island but the Depression came and things were pretty tough. Dad ordered six heifers from Prince Rupert. They weren't inspected very good and they had trouble with some disease that come up and got into the herd. It killed most of them. They only saved seven heifers. I was pretty small. In fact, one of the cows that survived, old Blue Bird, I was raised on her milk. I was big enough to go to the barn with Mother when she'd milk it. She'd set me right in the manger with her. And then later when I got big enough she'd set me up on top of the cow while she milked.

We had a good living. We had a good garden, chickens. Clams on the beach and deer in the woods, salmon and halibut, all we had to do was just go out and get them. And we made everything—jellies and jams. Everything was by hand. Mother canned a lot. She made everything, cottage cheese and several different types of cheese. Couldn't afford to eat a cow, because they were too precious. So it was eggs, cottage cheese and venison and seafood. All Mother would have to say is go out and fish, we need a fish or a halibut—or what ever she wanted. We'd go

William Stensland

get it. We had no way to keep it, outside of canning it, and salting it. Oh, and we smoked fish and lots of things.

As a boy we spent almost every summer at Helm Bay. I had a big 14-foot canoe and painted it red. That's the only paint we had, so we painted it red. Old Hansen, he wanted to make room on the dock at Sunde and d'Evers. Somebody had left the canoe there and it had a hole in it, it hit a rock or somethin'. Real nice canoe, but it was heavy. So he threw it off the dock and we were comin' along with the skiff and seen it floatin' and picked it up and took it home and patched it. And painted it and there was nothin' wrong with it. We had it for years. We'd hunt seal with it, and you'd be surprised how much game you'd see with it. Go paddlin' along the shore, just be quiet, goin' up in the creeks. You'd always see somethin'—porcupines or otter or mink or somethin' wherever you went. Couple times we even paddled up to a wolf on the point. There's a ridge of rocks that runs out there and there's a nice bay behind with a sand beach, and the wolf was right out on the tip of that rock. We paddled within 200 yards of him. When he finally seen us, he stood there broadside, like a picture, and then he decided to leave and he went over and jumped off that rock ridge and went in the woods. That great big black ol' wolf. If we'd had a decent gun we could have shot him.

At that time my brother Henry, he had a .30-.30 Remington and I don't know, there was somethin' wrong with his eyes or somethin' because every time he had a gun and I picked it up and shoot, it was three foot to one way or the other. I never could hit nothin' with his gun and I'm a good shot. He'd sight it in and he'd get his deer but by God we couldn't hit nothin' with it. We did better with a .22, get up close to somethin' and plink him in the eye.

Ol' Doc Dickinson would go out on the boat hunting and whatnot. And he'd always take one or two of us boys along to row the boat and do the work—dig clams, and man the crab pots, and the shrimp pots. We would just love doing that of course. And he always had guns and shells and stuff for us, and we could use them anytime we went hunting.

I was with ol' Doc Dickinson on the *Icsis*. There was Rudy Stahr, and Ed Jones was there, so was Jack Zollenrust and Dad. We were just sittin' down to dinner and this other boat come in. And the one guy went ashore in the skiff, pulled it up. The other two were still on the boat. We were just sittin' down to a big pot of beans and I went up on deck and hollered over. He said, "Look on the beach, there's a big deer there!" And I said, "Well, shoot him. Aren't you gonna shoot him?" He said somethin' about his partner took the gun. So I went and told Doc. It was big deer, a huge buck. So they all got their guns. My dad had an old worn out .30-.30, the bullets hit about halfway to the beach. They all lined up on the back deck and they started shooting. Well, the deer went around in circles. He looked this way, and they were hitting limbs and everything. Ol' Stahr, he emptied the gun not even aimin' he was so excited. It was hilarious.

Ol' Doc, he loaded up a .35 automatic, the one I used all the time. He said, "Let the boy shoot. Let the boy take a shot now." And finally they gave me a chance to get on the stern there and take a shot. Well, the first shot I clipped the cedar bough just above the deer. Then I used Kentucky windage and pulled down a little bit and down he went. So I jumped in the skiff and rowed in there to beat heck and I just got up to him. What you do is put your foot on the horns, see, and slit the throat from behind. And, man, that son-of-a-gun got up. I finally got his throat cut, and then I just backed off. Man, he tried to get back in the woods. I had a hell of time getting him in the skiff because he was heavy. Took him out to the boat and hung it up. And old Stahr says, "I got it." And old Zollenrust, he says, "No, I think I hit it." And ol' Doc, he says, "No. The boy hit it."

So Dad, he wasn't satisfied so he skinned that deer out. And he couldn't find no marks, no blood, no nothin'. So he said, "Well something had to kill that deer, something had to knock it down." So he skinned the head out and right at the base of the horns was that hard-nosed bullet—they're kind of copper-jacketed—that hit and just knocked him out is what it did. So that settled the dispute right there. The kid got it. So they quieted down and finished their beans.

Well, I used to like to help when they built the fish traps. I enjoyed climbing around like a monkey. I used to surprise them. One time I was on a rigging scow being towed by the *Celtic*. I crawled up along a tow line from the rigging scow up to the *Celtic*. Herb Vick

128

was the skipper, and he was just standing there with his head out the window. And so I just took and shimmied across the tow line and oh I guess it was about 50 or 60 feet, and I walked up into the wheelhouse and opened the door and stood alongside him. He kinda turned his head a little bit and looked and walked over and I stood and looked out the window. And pretty soon he turned around and said, "Where the hell did you come from?" I just scared the hell out of him. He said, "You were on the rigging scow." Then it dawned on him. He said, "How did you get over?"

I met my wife in a kinda roundabout way; my father-in-law bought the trolling boat *Ena*, down in Washington. He came to Alaska and went to Port Alexander to fish. Well I was going to Port Alexander to build a light on the rock outside the harbor. When I got out there I seen the *Ena* laying over there at anchor. So I went and rowed over there to the *Ena*, and I knocked on the door and my future father-in-law stuck his head out, and he asked me if there was anything he could do for me. I said I was looking for the owners of the boat, Mr. and Mrs. Ulick. "Oh," he said, "He don't own it anymore." He said he bought it from them in Seattle. So when I looked, there was a face peeking out every port hole. Five kids and mother and father-in-law-to-be and all the kids.

We were around there for a few days working on this light. and we went to town. We seen the girls. On Saturdays, the Navy boys would come over and they would sometimes put on the jukebox, and play some music. We went up there and got acquainted with everybody, and did some dancing, and took the girls over next door for some ice cream. I told Jo, my wife-to-be, "If you come to Ketchikan, you look me up or give me a phone call and we'll go to the show." Well that's what happened. So we got to going together and we got married.

We'd just come from spendin' the winter in Seattle about the first of March. I had a pretty good year. And Jo had always wanted to move back to Gravina. So we moved back. Mother hadn't been feeling good. So the first thing I did when I got back, I took and went out and set the set line at Gravina Point. There's a hole out there and I got several red snapper and I filleted 'em all up and I told Mom, "You just stay in bed and I'll cook dinner." There was a heck of a gang, couple older brothers and all my kids and some of the neighbor kids and Mother and Dad. Anyway, I fired up the old stove and cooked the meal, potatoes and red snapper and carrots and peas and stuff. The children had finished, they were playin' in the big front room and I'd been tellin' stories about the *kushtakas* and I'd shut the door, nice and dark in there. They were playin' and heard the cracklin' upstairs. Linda opened the door and she come runnin' in the kitchen. "Dad, Dad, the house is on fire!" I'd been workin' on my 18-horse Johnson, gettin' it ready, changin' plugs and greasin' it and whatnot, and I had a big fire extinguisher in the shed. I grabbed that and ran upstairs. And I could blow the flame out, but there was no water. Everything was froze, there was just enough runnin' in the kitchen for dishes and cookin' and stuff. So somebody bailed the back of the toilet tank, brought that up and we danged near got it out with that. If I'd had another bucket of water, we could have saved the house. But she'd broke through enough to get underneath.

There was a north wind blowin'. Cold. And the tide was way out. That real strong wind just blew right in there. And I managed to get some of the stuff out the upstairs window. I just threw it out. We had all our stuff stored up there, Jo and I. Mother had one bedroom that was just like a museum. She had gold scales and lots of Indian artifacts, paddles and little canoes and braided hats and baskets. Now it'd be museum stuff. And anyway, we just lost it. And the thing was, the same day we'd loaded the back room with canned goods—I was headed to Bristol Bay—and we got $200 worth of canned goods. And that was a lot of canned goods. Jo drew out a $1,000 and put $200 for groceries, and she had the rest of it in her wallet, in her jacket upstairs. I went by it, and I didn't know she had it in her pocket, $800. I threw a whole bunch of stuff out the top stair window. I could've threw it right out. I guess it feeds the fire in hell.

After we got through upstairs, my brother and I went into the kitchen and threw out a bunch of stuff. Mother had all the old pictures and stuff in the old phonograph case; that's where she kept her old pictures and records. By that time it was a ragin' inferno and I grabbed that phonograph case and handed it out to my sister-in-law

130

Betty. We had a bunch of wood blocks stacked up there, and I think I set it there and told Betty to take it. That's what I remember. What I should've done was throw it out in the yard. But we never could find that, never found the handle or anything. But the woodpile was still there. But anyway that was quite a loss—all my pictures that I'd taken before I went in the service and all through the service. So anyway we lost everything, goldarnit.

If you're on the water don't smoke. That's what I was trying to do, I was trying to light a cigarette when I hit a log.

We'd been over there [at Gravina], Gene Manaman, and my wife's sister and my dad. We had a picnic, a nice time and of course we had a few little toddies and stayed until just before dark. I was going to see how fast I could take them home and get back. I had the 50-horse Mercury on a 14-foot Boston Whaler, and gee whiz that thing flew. The handle control was broke and so I jury-rigged it. I grabbed a turn on the handle and away I'd go. I just run into Nordby's float and Gene and Jerry jumped out and I never shut the motor off and back across I went.

Well, when I come through the pass there at Snow's Island, it was just getting dark, enough so that you couldn't see very good. I decided to have a cigarette. So I bent down and held the edge of my coat up, so I could shelter my lighter for just long enough to light that goddamn cigarette and that's all it took—hit that log. It took the goldarned handle out of my hand. 'Course when I released it, then the engine went to idle. Man, I slid across and I went sailin' about 20 feet I guess. Just as pretty as you please. I thought, "Dammit, now I have to swim ashore and to get old Snow to take me home." I had just bought a new pair of short boots and I thought I had better take my new boots off—this is all going through my head—and I thought, "No by god, I just bought those damn things, I'm not going to kick my boots off." I was a pretty good swimmer, see, and I didn't want to lose my new boots. So I started for the shore and by that time it was dark.

I heard this *purrrrrrr*. Just a purring along. So I look over my shoulder, and here it's that goddamned boat coming in a big circle. But it took a little while for it to come around and I thought, "It's going to go between me and the beach. Well goddamn it, I'll just keep paddlin' and intercept it." But I tried too hard the first time—I was too anxious. I grabbed ahold of the bow, and my fingers just slipped off and I went down. I came up again. I got my arm underneath the back seat—they're real low back there, ya know. And when I reached up to pull myself in, of course my boots and everything weighed a lot, so I hung on to it like Christ sakes. I tried pulling myself up with just one arm, and I reached over and I got ahold of one of those cruiser tanks. I pulled enough weight that I pulled the damn hose off, that was the best thing I could do. She quit. And I went around the back, stepped on the motor and got in, stuck the hose in the tank, pumped it a few times and got home.

I come in the house and I was soaked, and well, here's Mom, Jo, my younger sister and the kids, and my brother Henry, they were all sitting there. And by gosh Mother laughed and the kids laughed. "Ha, ha, ha. Oh, Dad fell off the boom stick again!" Well, that was nothing to fall off the boom stick. You could always wade ashore, or walk ashore. or what ever. And I never did say a thing until the next morning, when I told Mom what happened. Oh my god, she had a fit.

We've been used to our freedom. When I was a boy, the bay was full of big old codfish, gee whiz, we'd go fish off the back porch. There were clams and deer, salmon and halibut, all we had to do was just go out and get them. But there's a bunch of educated idiots making laws. They need to hang on to some shrimp and clams and geoducks and seafood for the people that live here.

I like clams. I still go clamming or shrimping every chance I get. I'm going to do it until I die.

Josephine Stack Welfare

There's a curse that they have in old Kasaan.

Josephine Stack Welfare was born at Loring, Alaska, November 8, 1903. She was one of four daughters and five sons born to Richard and Mariah Stewart Stack, who married in Loring in 1894. Stack, originally of Oakland, California, was an Alaska Packers cannery supervisor; Mariah's Tsimshian family had emigrated from Old to New Metlakatla with Father Duncan in 1887. At the time of this interview in 1997, Jo Welfare was living in Kenmore, Washington. Her memories focused on her childhood in the bustling cannery town of Loring. "Aunt Jo," as she came to be known by the younger Stacks, died July 29, 1999.

Along the beach, people in tents, some of them from Metlakatla. Yeah, they build. And they had their wives with them, families. Some of them were Filipinos that lived out at Loring, too. They built little shacks or little tents towards the graveyard, down past Loring towards Indian Point. In the summer time, the cannery people used to bring their wives in there and all the women, they'd come in there and there'd be pregnant women. I don't know how many babies my mother delivered out at Loring!

The people from Metlakatla, they used to come over to see my mother. She used to like that because she could visit with them. She remembered Father Duncan. He did a lot of good for those Metlakatla people. He learned to talk Tsimshian. But she turned against him because he was against our dad. He didn't want the Metlakatla women to marry white people. But he ought to know that there wasn't enough Tsimpsians there, they'd be all inbred. But those people, they learned a lot. It was good for them that he was there.

133

Josephine Stack Welfare

When they come to Loring they could fish all along there. That's where I used to go trolling, catch fish. Yeah, salmon eggs, it's been a long time. And the kind my mother used to always get were the dog salmon. They was good. We used to say we had to let it ripen, they were called stink eggs. Did you ever try to eat them? I ate some of them.

My mother never wanted any of us to even get our feet wet. She was so afraid of us drowning. She had a cousin that drowned when he was young, and ever since that, she never wanted us to go near the water. But she let me go in the boat. They'd load the boat with humpies, whatever kind of fish they had. I would row it back to the beach, you know, where she would work on the fish.

Sometimes there'd be dog salmon there, you know. She used to split them and take out all of the insides and take it up to the smokehouse after she'd wash it with the salt water. She would hang them up there in the smokehouse overnight and the next day she would split them again, do whatever she had to do with it. She let it smoke, not let the heat get at it, just the smoke, don't know what she'd call it, but it had to be the right temperature.

Then she'd take the slices of fish and put them on a pole. We used to like that, we'd run around there eating them after they dried. She never let us cut anything. We just watched her do it.

She'd get the driftwood, always use the driftwood from the beach, that washed up on the beach, and the salt water. That's what she used to smoke with. She never used any fresh wood or anything, no alder, it had to be from the beach.

My dad used to, he'd save some fish when he was out brailing the traps, and he'd pick out fish that he wanted to take home and they let him do it. So she had enough for all winter. I used to like to sit out there at the smokehouse, especially in the evening.

The smokehouse was right out in back, you know where that walk goes and there's an outhouse there. But the smokehouse was up above that. Above the creek. Above the shed. The smokehouse was pretty big. Just for my family.

Yeah, I'd go over to the cannery when my dad would come. He'd tell us to watch for him, when he was coming in, and we'd go out on the porch, he'd call us to come on over, so I'd go alone in the

135

boat. When I think of it, I don't know how my mother trusted me so much. I must have been around 10 or something.

But Mags, my sister Maggie, she was two years older, she wouldn't go, she was scared. I went once with Mags and when you go by that big *Star of Greenland* [a square-rigged windjammer of the Alaska Packers fleet] or whichever one that was there, the waves would come in and you'd go up really close to that big iron ship. And Mags would be holding her breath. "Oh, don't go that close to it." But I said, "It's not going to hurt anything, we get on the other side of it, we get the fish and go back home."

But it was sometimes scary at the cannery. They used to have the Chinese and Mexicans there. They made all the cans, you know, and then they worked when the fish come in. But there was always so much trouble up there. I remember when I was working there, I was, I must have been about 16 or something like that, they had a stabbing up there, you know. Because they had telephone wire from Loring to Ketchikan, they called in right away and they sent this big Navy, it was the Navy at that time, they bring their marshal. One time one fellow was stabbed through the heart; they got that big artery, you know. He died before he got to Ketchikan.

Sometimes, just when we sit down to eat, then all of a sudden we'd hear that, they blow this whistle down at the cannery, on this big stack, you know. My mother, she would call us all come on in and stay in, there is something wrong. I remember when that happened, I think it was 1915, when my mother had us all come in, close the doors. She wouldn't light the lamps, you know, those kerosene lamps. She wouldn't turn them on till my dad came home, till he told us it was all right. We wanted to go pick berries but we were scared because of those Mexicans.

My sister Mags, she liked to go in the boats and get those gumboots, you know. That's what she liked to do. I never liked to do those. I never liked to eat them either. Yeah, she'd go to Donnelly Point. She wouldn't get her feet wet. But she liked to go and get the gumboots and what we call . . . candy canes, yeah . . . sea cucumbers.

And she liked to go berry picking. She'd go with my mother, they'd go in to Cache Island or somewheres around there. There was always a baby to take care of, and that's what I did. They'd bring home, oh, lots and lots of berries. They always brought me some of the branches with the berries on the branches so I have it. I used to eat the berries off the branches. My mother used to can all that, make jam.

Her favorite jams and jellies were blueberry and salal berries. Oh, they're good. We always say, "Well, when are the laughing berries going to be ripe?" They used to go to the island called Joe Island. The red huckleberries were on Cache Island. Elderberries, the old bachelors used to make wine out of them. There's the wild currants are good. They used to grow up there, up the lake on the way up to the hatchery. You know where Orton's property is down there. There used to be just loads of them along the river. Another thing that's real good, and I don't think there's very many people that's done much with them, is the wild crabapple. It's about the size of a cranberry.

The cranberry. Highbush cranberry. They never made jam or jelly out of it, but they'd fix it up their own way; they used ooligan oil. They had these wooden buckets like they used to use a lot in the old days. They used to eat that, put it on snow, when it snowed, like ice cream. I never liked it.

Oh, those were happy days! You know, as I think about it and talk about it now, all those days I can see so plain, so clear. The sun shining, that's just the way it is in my mind.

Doing my own trolling. That's when I caught my first fish. A 50-pound king salmon. It was a red king salmon. I remember I was trolling out around Loring and my dad was working up on the dock, building this big wharf for when the ship would come. So he seen that I had a salmon on my line. And he called to me, and I said, "Yes, I have a salmon but I can't get it in, it's too big!"

So he said, "You wait, just make the boat go around there and don't go ashore." So he come out there in another boat, and my dad got out there and he took it. He had the gaff, you know, and he got it in the boat. He says, "We're not going to take this home, there's a fish buyer there." And he says, "This your first big king salmon, and you can get whatever money you get for it." So I got four cents a pound, two dollars. I thought that was a lot of money!

137

All those people on the float came over there to see the fish that I caught. It was hard for them to believe that it weighed 50 pounds, that this little girl caught this big salmon. My dad, he was the beach foreman there. That big one, boy, it sure towed me around the bay. My mother said, "Well, the next one you get, maybe a smaller one, you can bring it home and we'll smoke it." So sure enough, the next one I caught was about 23 pounds and she smoked it. It was real good.

I baited my own hook with herring, fresh herring. And this fellow, I remember his name was, let's see what was his name, Oscar Haldane, and he showed me how to bait the hook and then how to make these little sticks and put it in the herring so it would spin and it looked like it was alive. That way the salmon would come and grab my bait.

I remember we went to old Kasaan. We had to go by boat. The Haida people were living there and they had a lot of totem poles. And my mother told me and Mags and she told my dad, "If you go ashore don't let Mags or Josephine touch anything. If the graves are open or anything don't let them go in there." So we went over there. And I remember there was this mate that my dad had on the boat with him. He was a mate off the big ship that brought up the sailors and all the crew every year. He went ashore with us and then this other lady that went with us was the beach boss's wife. They went up and went inside and they saw those little houses were the graves. Instead of putting the coffins underground, the Haidas just stacked them in these little log houses.

My dad told them, "You're not supposed to touch anything. Don't go in there or handle anything. If you do, there will be a curse on you." They handled it anyway.

I was scared, I must have been about 10. We went back to the boat. I remember I was praying, you know. When I got home I told my mother what happened. "Well," she said, "did you touch anything?" And I said, "No. I didn't even go in. Mags didn't either. We stayed away."

My mother said, "You watch, you just watch, something is going to happen to them or their families."

And it did that same year. This woman that was there, her brother drowned and the cook that was on that boat, he went along with my dad to go up to Traitors Cove; they were trying to get some crabs. The boat turned over, never found his body. He went in there.

And then the mate from the ship, why when he got back to San Francisco, he wasn't there a month or so, he died. They said he just died in his sleep. So there was three of them that went into that. My mother said, "You see, I wasn't trying to scare you kids. There's a curse that they have on anybody that will go into one of those places where they are buried."

It's just too bad, you know, how my brother George, how his eyes got bad. I can just see him now and I think about him sometimes, in the kitchen, it was that shelf, where they had the ketchup and different spices. George used to climb up, liked to get into things. And he pulled this can of cayenne pepper, right in his face and his eyes. And I remember, and I ran out there to see what was wrong. And he was screaming and I tried to pick him up and he kicked at me and I asked him what's the matter, and he told me that pepper got in his eyes. So I called my mother, I don't know what she was doing, or whether she was fixing the smoked salmon. I was always taking care of the baby. Mags was always around doing the cooking, but when it come to taking care of the kids, I was always the one. And, oh, he just about tore my dress up, he was in so much pain. So my dad came home from work and my mother told him what had happened. He said what did you do for it. She said Jo was the only one in the kitchen with him, and I told him all I did was put water. Well, that's the best you could do, I guess, he says, there's nothing else.

Took him to a doctor in Ketchikan and all that, and they said there was nothing they could do for him. That's why he never went to school a day in his life. I used to feel sorry, he used to sit up on that big porch when we'd go to school, and he'd be looking down there. Yeah, but he couldn't see anything. He had these big bandages around his eyes all the time. He had a bad temper after that. My dad said he had a brother George, and he had a bad temper, too. So all my mother could do was give him some bark from the alder tree. And she fixed him up pretty good. His eyes got so he could see, but not good enough to go to school.

I haven't thought about that for a long time, and now that I think of it, I haven't thought of a lot of these things, but I can see them all.

Emma Williams

The old people got together, and my marriage was all planned when I got home

Emma Williams, a Tlingit, was the youngest child of George and Maggie Kininnook. She was born in Metlakatla June 22, 1898, and spent her early childhood in Ketchikan. After her father died in an accident in 1905, Emma, her mother and a sister spent time with grandparents in Wrangell. They were in Ketchikan again when her mother died in 1912, two weeks after Emma's 14th birthday. Emma, alone, was looked after by relatives until her arranged marriage to Frank Williams in 1915 in Metlakatla, where they lived until they bought a home in Ketchikan in 1924. This interview was in March 1996. Emma died February 15, 1998, at age 99.

My father's name was George Paul Kininnook. My mother's was Maggie Kininnook. We lost my father when I was still small age. I just don't barely remember him. He was helping an old lady . . . he used to work by the creek . . . low tide. And they were going to work on the roof of her house because she was the Widow Swanson, Mrs. Swanson. And they forgot to nail the scaffolds down and they walked to the one side, the plank tipped with him and he fell to the rocks below.

My grandmother, her name was Emma, was married to a man in Wrangell, so she had a home there. She didn't want mama to have a hard time with us, so Grandfather came down to take us to Wrangell, and that's where we lived, was Grandma's house. She took care of us, Mama and me, and my sister Maud.

We used to go up the Stikine River, they had a nice cabin up there, springtime. Grandma used to just love it. The place that Grandpa came, they called it "clear water." It run into the Stikine really clear.

Emma Williams

They could get some fish to dry for our winter use. Twice a year Grandma loved to go up there. Then, Mama, she wanted to come back, we were more grown up now, so we moved back here to Ketchikan.

It was just a small town then. Down there where Thomas Basin is now, it was just like a bay and a long run-out beach. There was no sidewalk. There was a narrow path along the upper side of the creek. And people walked on the beach. And our native people began to move here, build their houses there. That's how I remember it. That was way back.

For myself, I have to tell this much. My mother got sick and she was already sick in bed. William Dickinson, he was a jailer, a native, but his wife died so he let us live in his house on the first floor. My sister and I tried to take care of our mother. She was sick. I wondered one day why she kept sending me back to town. "You go get this for me," she said. And she tells me what she wants and I go. The third time I came, she was sitting up in bed. There was a little table by the side of her bed. And there was a cake! It was my 14th birthday, she was celebrating. I was so happy, my 14th year.

My (older) sister and another lady they went for dancing with their husbands. And Mama looks at me, she open her eyes. I was sitting in the rocking chair by her bedside, and she said, "Give me my tie." And I said, "What for, Mama?" We were talking our language. "Don't you know today is a holiday? I want to use it." And that's her last words to me. And she went to sleep.

Some man came in, he walked over, looked down at Mama, "I'm going after my mother," he said, and he ran down the steps. I could hear him. In a little while I could hear people running up the steps . . . started to calling, "Mama, Auntie," in our language. She never spoke. She died, 9:30 Fourth of July night. Fourth of July was no holiday for me for a long time. I was sitting by her bedside.

I was left alone. We went to, they moved us out to Cholmondeley, that's where the big cannery was, and that's where I lived with my brother's wife in a tent. David Kininnook and his wife Sarah. And we used to work, start work in the cannery at six o'clock in the morning. I don't know how long we worked. All we got was 25 cents an hour at that time, at the end $94. I don't know how I did it, but I did it.

Then this lady, Mary Kyan, she's been to the Chemawa School in Oregon. She kept talking to me, "You better come with us, what will you do this winter?" I said, "Gee, we never went to school except for a little time in Wrangell." There were a lot of kids from Hydaburg, Klawock. We rode on the Alaska Steamship to Seattle, and on the train, with Mary Kyan to the school. I sign up for five years. I start the fourth grade and passed the fifth grade.

And my sister kept writing for me, I'm lonesome for you, you can always go back. My marriage was all planned when I got home. I guess, when before I got home, the old people got together on Frank's side and my side's grandparents. I didn't even know him. I didn't know what to do. I had nobody to talk for. My sister couldn't talk for me. I told them, "I signed up for five years at school." But the old people was so strong, my grandparents and Frank's side, so I had to give in. I was going on 17. I didn't make enough money in cannery, so I just had to give in, I guess.

His name was Frank M. Williams. We lived in Metlakatla and we lived together, married for 64 years. We got married by the Tsimshian minister Edward Marsden, who was married to my oldest sister, Lucy. You know what we had for our meal? Corn beef soup for our wedding meal. Decided Frank belonged to the women, helped his mother to make the stew, and crackers, wedding cake. That's all we had.

We lived over there with Frank's parents, tried to do like the old customs years back, when they get married they have to live with their family. But that was out in the villages and they called it family house. Oh, I never realize how hard I worked. Frank had three sisters and one brother still going to school. I don't how I managed it, but I was young. I have to get lunch ready for them coming home from school.

One day when they come running home, hanging down from their jackets on a string was little red tags, on it was written "I speak English" on those red tags. And they don't allow anybody to use our language on the school ground. If they catch you, you lose your tag. In Metlakatla they had government schools over there. And that's how they start to lose the language. They got punished when they hear them speaking our own language.

We bought this house on Stedman Street in 1924, October, when we moved here to Ketchikan. Still there, blue house across from radio station. Eleanor she was five.

I had my two daughters, Eleanor—she was pianist for the church—and I had Frances. My husband, he was a fisherman, but he learned what his father taught him, to fish, trapping, hunting.

When we lived with my grandmother she taught us how to beadwork. And I make money on it. I picked it up but my sister Maud, she was four years older, wasn't interested in it—making moccasins. And when we lived here I taught making moccasins and one year I taught at the Heritage Center. I had seven women I taught beadwork, two weeks at a time. I just taught two years. I didn't want to pay too much income tax. That was recent time.

One year a long time ago we had a really hard time. Depression. Working in cannery, getting only 35 cents an hour. I used to just walk down from my house to the cannery, started at six o'clock in the morning. We were at the fish table, where they pack them in cans.

At home I canned salmon in the jars, salted them in the barrel. And we used to move out to smoke them. Wild berries in the summer, put them up in jars—jam, jelly.

Another hard time. I had a little baby boy, it was healthy boy, five weeks. And a little pimple came out between his little shoulders in the back. And he was fussy, to cry, and my husband called the doctor. And he opened his satchel. He took out his instrument and he lanced that pimple open. Poor baby screamed, you could hear him down the street. I left the house, I didn't want to see, I could hear my baby screaming from down the street. And the baby never stopped bleeding, he just bled to death. I don't know why he had that pimple come up. I didn't have no choice, so I lost my baby. Five weeks old. Lot of times I think about him, if he had lived, he might have been here to take care. It was no peaceful days for me for months. So I didn't have any more children after that.

We used to just walk down to the church, it was right across from the [federal] building, the Presbyterian church. When Frances was a little bigger I used to wheel her down in the buggy. She was a good baby, good in church.

Oh, one time, a doctor pulled my wisdom tooth and next morning I couldn't open my jaw. It locked my jaws. I had to go to the hospital, the old hospital. I couldn't eat. All the sisters used to come— orange juice, fresh milk, potatoes mashed in a little cup. I had no neck, it was straight down swollen so big. Ten days . . . it's so painful. After awhile a doctor's nurse comes in and says she's going to give me a big hypo. I was just thinking to myself, I wonder what she's doing that for. Well, maybe this is the night. I just knocked out. In the morning one nurse came in and throw her arms around me and says, "Mrs. Williams, you're all right now." Another nurse comes in and says, "You're all right now." I started to keep moving my jaw. Oh, it was bitter in my mouth.

During the war we had those blackout papers to cover the windows. And when I went down the stores were sold out. All I could get was for my kitchen. It's scary when the whistle start to blow. When you look out it's pitch dark. Frances, she open the door just a little bit, and that man standing by the radio station [across the road], he says, "Close that door!" It was kind of scary.

World War II we had no stockings to buy, no house dresses to buy. They told us to use old dress-up dress. No bacon, no eggs, no crackers. But we managed, what we can get from stores. We used Mother's Oats for potatoes. I don't know what we used in place of meat. It was so long ago I forgot now. Not real butter, it looked like tallow. Mix up that little yellow package with it, but it's yellow after we mix that little package. It didn't taste like real butter.

Some rough times. Frank died, I don't remember the year now [1979]. It was a happy marriage. But he was a very jealous-hearted man. I was good looking, I guess. I never drank. I never went to dances because my husband didn't know how to dance, I was taken off the floor. And so we just lived a happy life. We weren't cold, we weren't hungry, we lived together.

I am now 97 years old. My birthday is June 22, and I pray that God spare my life, I'll reach that age 98.

146